D0041299

BERNIE SANDERS

GUIDE TO POLITICAL REVOLUTION

BERNIE SANDERS

GUIDE TO POLITICAL REVOLUTION

WITH ILLUSTRATIONS BY **JUDE BUFFUM**

GODWINBOOKS

Henry Holt and Company ★ New York

Henry Holt and Company, *Publishers since 1866*

Henry Holt® is a registered trademark of Macmillan Publishing Group, LLC

175 Fifth Avenue, New York, NY 10010 • fiercereads.com

Text copyright © 2017 by Bernie Sanders

Illustrations copyright © 2017 by Jude Buffum

All rights reserved.

Library of Congress Cataloging-in-Publication Data is available.

ISBN 978-1-250-13890-3

Our books may be purchased in bulk for promotional, educational,
or business use. Please contact your local bookseller or the Macmillan
Corporate and Premium Sales Department at (800) 221-7945 ext. 5442
or by e-mail at MacmillanSpecialMarkets@macmillan.com.

First edition, 2017 / Book design by April Ward

Based on the book *Our Revolution: A Future to Believe In* by Bernie Sanders,
published by Thomas Dunne Books, an imprint of St. Martin's Press.

Printed in the United States of America

1 3 5 7 9 10 8 6 4 2

I want to dedicate this book to the younger generation. You are, in many ways, the most progressive generation in the history of our country. You have opposed racism, sexism, homophobia, xenophobia, and oligarchy. You understand that greed and the grotesque level of income and wealth inequality that we experience is not what the United States is supposed to be about. You know that climate change is real, and that we have a moral responsibility to take on the fossil fuel industry and transform our energy system away from fossil fuel and into energy efficiency and sustainable energy.

What this book is about is converting that idealism and generosity of spirit into political activity. And when you do that, I have no doubt but that you and others like you will create a lot better world than the one my generation left you.

In solidarity,

BERNIE SANDERS

★ THE AGENDA

FOREWORD

I am proud of my campaign for president and that, in the Democratic primary, taking on virtually the entire party establishment, we won 22 states and over 13 million votes. I am proud that we funded the campaign not through super PACs but through millions of small donations averaging $27, and that grassroots activists—not politicians—played a major role in our successes.

I am especially proud that, in virtually every state primary and caucus, we won the overwhelming majority of young people—black, white, Latino, Asian American, and Native American. In fact, my campaign received more votes from young people than Donald Trump's and Hillary Clinton's combined.

The young people of this country are, of course, the future of America. And that bodes well for us. It is my observation that the current generation of young people is the smartest, most idealistic, and least preju-diced generation in the modern history of the United States. This is a generation that is prepared to think big and move this country in a very different direction than we have been traveling for years. It is especially pre-pared to reject the value system espoused by Donald Trump and the right-wing reactionaries in Congress who support his ideas.

The basic thesis of this book is pretty simple. It is that, on major issue after major issue, the vast majority of Americans support a progressive agenda and widely reject the economic views of the Republican Party. Go into any community in this country—including in the most conservative states—and you'll not find many peo-ple who think that it makes sense to give hundreds of billions in tax breaks to the top 1 percent while at the same time cutting Social Security, Medicare, Medicaid, education, and health care. You'll not find many peo-ple who think climate change is a "hoax." But those are the ideas that President Trump and most of the Republican leadership in Congress support.

On the other hand, most Americans believe it's imperative that we raise the minimum wage to a living wage, that we guarantee pay equity for women, and that we join the rest of the world in guaranteeing paid family and medical leave. The American people under-stand that health care is a right for all and not a privilege, and that in a competitive global economy we must make public colleges and universities tuition-free. They want us to create millions of good-paying jobs by rebuilding our crumbling infrastructure and by investing in sustainable energy and affordable housing.

The American people know that in the midst of massive wealth and income inequality the very rich have got to start paying their fair share of taxes, and that we desperately need reforms to our broken immigration and criminal justice systems. They understand that women must have the right to control their own bodies, and that we must move aggressively to combat racism, sexism, and homophobia.

That's not Bernie Sanders talking. That's what poll after poll shows the American people want.

Well, you might ask, if that's true, then why do Republicans now control the White House, the Senate, the House of Representatives, and almost two-thirds of the governors' offices throughout the country? Why are they completely in control—the governorship, the state house, and the state senate—in half of the states?

Great question, and that's what this book is all about.

In my view, if we are to successfully address the enormous problems now facing our country and planet, we need to understand that democracy is not a spectator sport. We can no longer sit back and allow ourselves to have one of the lowest voter turnouts of any major country on earth. We can no longer allow the wealthy and their campaign contributions to determine the future of our government. We must move boldly forward to revitalize American democracy and bring millions of young people and working people into an unstoppable political movement that fights for a government that represents all of us, not just the billionaire class.

And that's what I am now beginning to see in communities across the country. By the millions, people are taking to the streets in opposition to Trump's reactionary agenda. They are standing up for health care, for women's rights, for the environment, and to protect Social Security and retirement benefits. They are fighting to make college affordable, and for decent wages and working conditions for America's workers.

They are also starting to run for political office. Sometimes it's the local school board or city council or mayor's office. Sometimes it's the state house. Sometimes it's for the U.S. House or Senate.

That momentum must continue, and it must expand. This is your country. Help us take it back. Join the Political Revolution.

★ ONE

GUARANTEEING A LIVABLE WAGE AND A DECENT LIFE

THE MINIMUM WAGE MUST BECOME A LIVING WAGE

In the wealthiest country in the history of the world, a basic principle of American economic life should be that if you work forty hours or more a week, you do not live in poverty.

Sadly, that is far from reality.

More than forty-three million Americans are living in poverty today. Many of those people actually work, but they are still below the federal poverty level. Meanwhile, health care costs are going up, child care costs are going up, college costs are going up, and housing costs are going up. But wages are not. Low-income workers need a significant boost in what they earn if they are going to live with dignity in today's economy.

The current federal minimum wage of $7.25 an hour is a starvation wage. The minimum wage must become a living wage—which means raising it to $15 an hour by 2020 and tying it to cost-of-living increases in the future. And we must also close the loophole that allows employers to pay workers who get tips—waiters, waitresses, bartenders, barbers, hairdressers, taxi drivers, car wash assistants, valet parking attendants—a shamefully low $2.13 an hour.

These changes would benefit more than seventy-five million workers and their families. It would help to address racial inequity, giving a boost to the 54 percent of African American workers and nearly 60 percent of Hispanic workers who earn less than $15 an hour. According to the most recent statistics, women make up nearly two-thirds of all minimum-wage workers. Increasing the minimum wage would also significantly boost the wages of more than fifteen million women currently making above minimum wage but less than $15 an hour.

In some places, the American people are demanding change. The cities of Seattle, Los Angeles, San Francisco, New York, and Washington, D.C., are all raising the minimum wage to $15 an hour. The states of California and New York, two of the largest in our country, did the same. As a result of these efforts, ten million workers in America will see their wages raised to $15 an hour.

This not only helps the ten million workers who get a pay raise but also provides a much-needed boost to our economy.

One measure of a country's economic health is its gross domestic product, the value of all the goods produced in the country and the services provided by its citizens in a year. Today, 70 percent of our GDP is dependent upon the purchasing power of consumers. If millions of American workers have no money available to purchase goods and services, the economy falters.

On the other hand, when low-wage workers have money in their pockets, they spend that money in grocery stores, restaurants, and businesses throughout

★ ★ ★

In the richest country in the history of the world, our people should not be living in such despair and hopelessness.

TWEET BY BERNIE SANDERS, APRIL 19, 2017, 11:23 AM

There's no state where a full-time minimum wage worker can afford a one-bedroom apartment at the fair market rent. That's unacceptable.

TWEET BY BERNIE SANDERS, APRIL 10, 2017, 3:51 PM

this country. All this new business gives companies a reason to expand and hire more workers. This is a win-win-win for our economy. Poverty is reduced. New jobs are created. And we reduce the skyrocketing income inequality that currently exists in this country.

Every time a minimum wage increase is proposed locally or nationally, conservative politicians and their billionaire campaign contributors claim that jobs will be destroyed. Time and time again they have been proven dead wrong.

After San Jose, California, increased its minimum wage to $10 an hour in March 2013, fast-food restaurants did not lay off workers—they added workers. In fact, by 2014, employment gains in San Jose exceeded the job growth in the rest of the state.

San Francisco experienced impressive job gains in the food service industry after first raising its minimum wage in 2004. According to researchers at the University of California, Berkeley, between 2004 and

2011, restaurant employment increased nearly 18 percent in San Francisco, while nearby counties in the Bay Area without the higher standard saw only 13 percent growth.

In January 2014, SeaTac, Washington, became the first town in America to raise its minimum wage to $15 an hour—which meant an immediate 63 percent pay increase for low-wage workers. Before this pay raise took effect, business owners warned of massive layoffs.

Scott Ostrander, general manager of Cedarbrook Lodge in SeaTac at the time, said that he would be forced to shut down part of the hotel, eliminate jobs, and reduce the hours of his workforce. But after the minimum wage was raised, business was so good that the hotel moved ahead with a $16 million expansion and hired more workers.

A Seattle restaurateur similarly warned that the higher minimum wage could force him to shut down restaurants. Instead, he announced that he would be opening five new restaurants in Seattle.

Increasing the minimum wage is good for businesses as well as workers because it reduces employee turnover. When workers earn a living wage, they are more likely to stay with their company.

A January 2015 poll by Hart Research Associates shows 63 percent of Americans support raising the minimum wage to $15 an hour. It's not just what the American people want. Many economists support raising the minimum wage.

Why do the taxpayers of this country pay billions of dollars a year for programs such as SNAP (Supplemental Nutrition Assistance Program, commonly known as the food stamp program), Medicaid, and subsidized housing? The answer is clear. Millions of American workers need these programs because they cannot survive on the starvation wages their employers pay. Public assistance given to low-wage workers is essentially subsidizing the profits of the companies paying the low wages. Those corporations and all businesses should be paying their employees wages that they can live on with dignity, without the need for public assistance.

Consider Walmart. The Walton family, the owners of Walmart, is the wealthiest family in the country, with an estimated net worth of more than $130 billion. This one family owns more wealth than the combined wealth of the bottom 42 percent of Americans—130 million people. It also receives more welfare than anybody else.

Walmart makes profits by paying wages so low that the workers not only qualify for but also need public assistance just to get by. Many Walmart employees rely on Medicaid for health insurance for themselves and their children—paid for by the taxpayers of America. To feed their families, many Walmart workers receive food stamps—paid for by the taxpayers of America. And to keep a roof over their heads, many Walmart employees live in subsidized housing—paid for by the taxpayers of America. When you add it all up, American taxpayers spend at least $6.2 billion each year supporting Walmart employees, and therefore subsidizing Walmart profits, according to a 2014 report from Americans for Tax Fairness.

Walmart claims it cannot afford to pay its workers $15 an hour, but in 2015, its chief executive officer was paid more than $19.8 million (that works out to more than $9,500 an hour for a forty-hour work week), and it made nearly $15 billion in profits. If Walmart had paid all its workers at least $15 an hour in that same year, it would still have made a profit of over $10 billion. The Walton family has to get off welfare. It must pay workers a living wage.

Another major welfare recipient in this country is the fast-food industry and its owners. Taxpayers spend about $7 billion a year subsidizing the low wages of fast-food companies like McDonald's, Burger King, Wendy's, and many others.

From 2009 to 2011, taxpayers spent nearly $153 billion each year subsidizing companies that pay workers inadequate wages, according to a 2015 report from the UC Berkeley Center for Labor Research and Education.

I believe that the government has a moral

responsibility to provide for the vulnerable—the children, the elderly, the sick, and the disabled. But I do not believe that the government should burden taxpayers with the financial support of profitable corporations owned by some of the wealthiest people in this country. That's absurd.

And then there's the largest low-wage employer in America. It's not Walmart, McDonald's, or Burger King. The largest low-wage employer in America is the United States government.

Today, nearly two million Americans work at low-wage jobs funded by the taxpayers of our country, mainly through government contracts with private-sector employers to provide necessary services. That's more than the number of low-wage workers at Walmart and McDonald's combined.

These low-wage employees manufacture uniforms for the U.S. military. They repair our highways, sidewalks, and bridges. They work in gift shops at some of our national parks. They serve us breakfast and lunch in park cafeterias. They provide care for the elderly, the sick, and the disabled through government programs. They are the security guards who protect federal buildings and the employees who work there. They are janitors and groundskeepers who clean government office buildings, take out garbage, and mow lawns. The companies that hire these workers receive a contract from

the federal government, and in too many instances those employers are not paying a living wage.

In 2014, Barack Obama's administration signed an executive order requiring federal contract workers to be paid at least $10.10 an hour. But while that was a step in the right direction, much more needs to be done. In my view, we need a new executive order to increase the minimum wage for federal contract workers to a living wage of $15 an hour.

Raising the minimum wage benefits the economy, and it benefits society as a whole. There's a clear connection between poverty, despair, and crime. According to a recent report by President Obama's Council of Economic Advisers, "Higher wages for low-skilled workers reduce both property and violent crime, as well as crime among adolescents. The impact of wages on crime is substantial. . . . A 10 percent increase in wages for non-college educated men results in approximately a 10 to 20 percent reduction in crime rates."

When wages go up, crime goes down, and everyone benefits.

There is also a direct correlation between healthy babies and higher wages. Poverty causes stress, which can have long-term health consequences. Researchers at the University of Iowa, the University of Illinois at

Chicago, and Bentley University found that every $1 increase in the minimum wage was associated with a 2 percent reduction in the risk of a mother having a baby with a low birth weight. (Low birth weight means a hard beginning for a child. It can affect intellectual and physical development for many years—perhaps permanently.)

When wages go up, community health improves, and everyone benefits.

The bottom line is not complicated. No full-time worker should live in poverty. We must raise the minimum wage to $15 an hour.

EQUAL PAY FOR EQUAL WORK

Today, women make up nearly half of the U.S. workforce. Yet the average woman working full-time in this country still earns just 80 cents for every dollar a man makes doing the same job.

The gender pay gap is even worse for women of color. African American women earn just 63 cents, Hispanic women earn 54 cents, and Native American women only 58 cents for every dollar a white man earns.

Since the 1990s, more women have received

GENDER PAY GAP

White women earn **79 cents** to the white male dollar. *

Black women earn **63 cents** to the white male dollar.

Native American women earn **58 cents** to the white male dollar.

Hispanic women earn **54 cents** to the white male dollar.

*controlled for type of work and level of position

undergraduate and graduate degrees than men. In spite of these gains, the gender pay gap has remained roughly the same for the past fifteen years.

Equal pay is not just a woman's issue; it is also a family issue. When women do not receive equal pay for equal work, families across America have less money to spend on child care, groceries, and housing.

For millions of families across America, the pay gap between men and women can be the difference between being able to pay the hospital bill and going without needed medical care. It can be the difference between being able to pay the heating bill and being cold in the winter. And it can be the difference between paying the mortgage and losing a home to foreclosure.

We have to stop penalizing women in the workplace who have children. New mothers should receive the same respect and pay on the job that men receive when they are about to become fathers. According to a recent study from the University of Massachusetts Amherst, when men become fathers, their earnings go up by 6 percent. What happens to women? For every child they have, their income goes down by 4 percent. That is absurd.

MAKING IT EASIER FOR WORKERS TO JOIN UNIONS

If we are serious about reducing income and wealth inequality and rebuilding the middle class, we have to substantially increase the number of union jobs in this country. We must make it easier, not harder, for workers to join unions. The benefits of joining a union are clear:

★ Union workers earn 25 percent more, on average, than nonunion workers.

★ More than 81 percent of union workers have guaranteed defined-benefit pension plans, while only 18 percent of nonunion workers do. These pension plans calculate a pension by years worked and salary at the time of retirement.

★ More than 86 percent of workers in unions have paid sick leave, compared with just 65 percent of nonunion workers.

Today, just 11 percent of all public-sector workers belong to unions, and in the private sector it is now less than 7 percent. Historically, unions have enabled workers to earn good wages and work in decent conditions because of collective bargaining. Today, millions of workers are in a "take it or leave it" situation, with no power to influence their wages or benefits.

There is no question that one of the most significant reasons for the forty-year decline in the size of the middle class is that the rights of workers to join together and bargain for better wages, benefits, and working conditions have been severely undermined.

PAID FAMILY AND MEDICAL LEAVE

When it comes to supporting real family values, the United States lags behind every other major country on earth. We are the only advanced economy that doesn't guarantee its workers some form of paid family leave, paid sick leave, or paid vacation time. About 23 percent of working mothers in America have to go back to work just two weeks after giving birth. Just two weeks to bond and spend time with their newborn. In some cases, this is a matter of life and death. The United States has the highest infant mortality rate in the industrialized world. A recent study by researchers at UCLA and McGill University found that every additional month of paid family leave can reduce the infant mortality rate by 13 percent.

PAID FAMILY
AND MEDICAL LEAVE

In France, mothers are guaranteed at least **4 months** of paid maternity leave at up to **100%** of their wages.

In Canada, working parents are eligible for **35 weeks** of parental leave at up to **55%** of their salary.

In Japan, parents are guaranteed **1 year** of paid leave after a child is born, the first six months at up to **67%** of their salary, the remainder at **50%**.

In Germany, parents are guaranteed **1 year** of paid leave at up to **67%** of their salary.

In Norway, working parents who have a baby are entitled to **49 weeks** of paid leave at **100%** of their wages.

The Family and Medical Leave Act that Congress passed in 1993 is totally inadequate for our twenty-first-century workforce. The act requires some employers to provide workers up to twelve weeks of unpaid leave for personal or family illness, military leave, pregnancy, adoption, or the foster care placement of a child. However, it covers only employees in companies with fifty or more employees, and it requires only unpaid, rather than paid, leave. More than 40 percent of all American workers are not even covered by the law because they work less than twenty-four hours a week, have not worked for the company for twelve months, or work for companies with fewer than fifty employees. And nearly eight out of ten workers who are covered by the Family and Medical Leave Act and are theoretically eligible to take time off cannot afford to do so. In my view, every worker in America should be guaranteed at least twelve weeks of *paid* family and medical leave.

Today it would cost the average worker more than $9,300 in lost wages to take twelve weeks of unpaid leave. Most workers simply do not have that kind of money. In fact, according to a December 2015 survey, 63 percent of Americans do not even have $500 in their bank accounts to pay for an unexpected medical emergency or needed car repair.

The economic benefits of paid family and medical

leave more than outweigh the very modest costs of this program.

Women who have paid family leave are more likely to stay in the workforce and off federal programs like Medicaid, food stamps, and public housing.

Families that have paid leave are much less likely to declare bankruptcy.

And children have a greater chance of leading healthy and more productive lives if their parents have paid family leave.

The good news is that California, New Jersey, Rhode Island, Washington, and New York have all passed laws guaranteeing paid family and medical leave to workers.

California and New Jersey guarantee workers six weeks of paid family and medical leave, and in Rhode Island workers are eligible for four weeks of paid leave. In 2021, New York will become the first state in the nation to offer workers twelve weeks of paid family and medical leave.

PAID SICK LEAVE FOR ALL

We have to make sure that workers in this country have paid sick time. Forty-three million Americans don't have access to paid sick leave today.

In my view, it is insane that low-wage workers must work when they are sick because they cannot afford to stay home.

It's bad for the workers who are sick and unable to get the medical treatment they need to get better. It's bad for their employers, since a sick worker will be less productive for longer without appropriate medical treatment. And it is a public health issue, forcing sick individuals into public spaces where they risk spreading disease.

AMERICAN WORKERS NEED A VACATION

Millions of Americans are overworked, underpaid, and under enormous stress. Some are working two or three jobs to try to care for their families. Research shows that vacations reduce stress, strengthen family relationships, increase productivity, and even prevent illness. But 41 percent of workers didn't take one day of vacation in 2015.

One factor is the benefit of paid vacation time. Twenty-seven percent of all American workers get no paid vacation time. This disproportionately affects workers in low-wage jobs, of whom about 50 percent get no paid vacation time.

Americans are working more hours than the people of any other major developed country, including Japan, Germany, Canada, the United Kingdom, France, and Italy. They need time to rest and recuperate, travel the country, visit loved ones, or simply spend time at home with their families.

According to the Organization for Economic Cooperation and Development, in 2015 an average American worked 419 hours more than an average German worker, 308 hours more than a French worker, 125 hours more than an Australian worker, 116 hours more than a British worker, 84 hours more than a Canadian worker, and 71 hours more than a Japanese worker.

In my view we need legislation to require employers to provide at least ten days of paid vacation to workers in this country every year. This is not a radical idea. It is already being done in almost every country

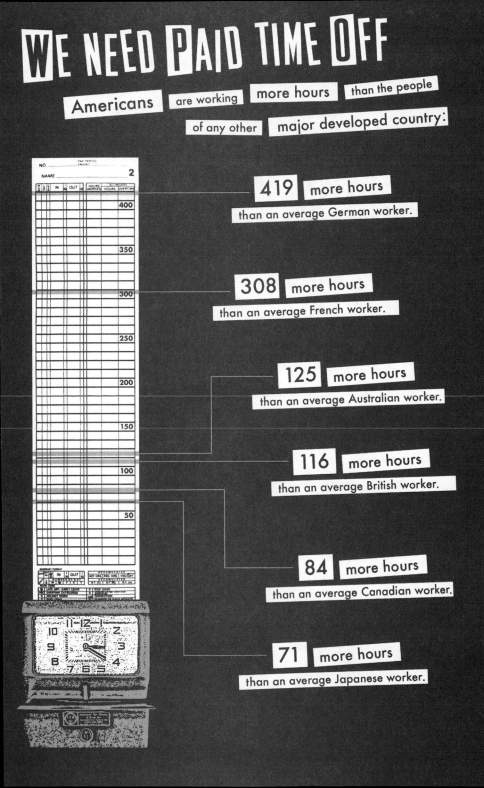

in the world. This would not only demonstrate our national commitment to family values but also make good economic sense. Studies show that paid-vacation policies boost productivity and worker loyalty.

JOBS, JOBS, JOBS
CREATING A FULL-EMPLOYMENT ECONOMY

In a modern democratic society, people have the right to a decent job at decent pay. There are enormous needs in this country that must be addressed. Let's put the unemployed and underemployed to work transforming America. Let's create a full-employment economy.

Today, real unemployment is not 5 percent. Including those who have given up looking for work, or who are working part-time when they want to work full-time, real unemployment is just over 9 percent. In many communities around the country, the unemployment rate is even higher than that. And it is tragically high among young people who are not college graduates. Today, it is estimated that about twenty million Americans are unemployed or underemployed and that only 63 percent of the adult population has a job.

If we are serious about reversing the decline of the middle class, we need a major federal jobs program that puts millions of Americans to work at decent-paying jobs.

We need workers to rebuild our crumbling infrastructure—our roads, bridges, water systems, wastewater plants, airports, railways, levees, and dams.

We need workers to help us lead the world in combating climate change by making our homes and buildings more energy-efficient and transforming our energy system away from fossil fuels and to sustainable energy. We will also need a twenty-first-century electric grid capable of transmitting that energy.

We need workers to help us address the crisis in affordable housing—making certain that every family in America lives in a safe and affordable space. This means not only building millions of units of new housing but also rebuilding the older housing stock in communities throughout the country.

We need workers to create a modern pre-K and child care system worthy of the youngest Americans and their parents.

We need workers to make certain that our children attend modern, well-constructed schools. And we need the best and brightest of our young people to enter the teaching profession so that our kids get a world-class education.

We need workers to build, in every community in America, urban and rural, a high-quality broadband network. In the modern world, broadband is a necessity, not a luxury.

We need more doctors, nurses, dentists, and other medical personnel to provide quality health care to all as a right. There are medically underserved areas in large cities, small towns, and rural regions where millions of Americans, even those with insurance, are unable to access the health care they need.

We need to make it easier for the entrepreneurial spirit to flourish. That means providing help to those businesses that really need it, not to large and profitable corporations that are shipping our jobs abroad.

MOBILIZE ★ ★ ★

STAND WITH WORKERS

Recently, workers at McDonald's, Burger King, Wendy's, Popeyes, and other fast-food establishments stood up and fought for justice. They demonstrated, they took to the streets, and even though they do not officially belong to a union, they had the courage to go out on strike in New York City, Detroit, Flint, Chicago, St. Louis, Kansas City, Washington, D.C., and dozens of other cities. Support vocal workers by standing with them if possible, or at least refuse to cross a picket line.

If you or anyone you know is working under a federal contract and experiencing wage theft—not being paid the wage guaranteed by law or receiving guaranteed benefits—contact Good Jobs Nation at goodjobsnation .org or 1-844-PAY-FAIR.

If you support a living wage for workers, sign a petition on fightfor15.org.

EQUAL PAY FOR EQUAL WORK

The mission of the American Civil Liberties Union is to protect individual rights and liberties guaranteed by the U.S. Constitution. Its Women's Rights Project focuses litigation, advocacy, and public education on reforming institutional discrimination against women. Its site, aclu.org/issues/womens-rights, outlines the current challenges and provides links to news and videos.

More women in elected office will mean more voices for all women. Support Emily's List, emilyslist.org, in its efforts to inform voters about female candidates.

GIVE YOUR TIME

AmeriCorps (nationalservice.gov) engages more than 80,000 Americans in intensive service each year at non-profits, schools, public agencies, and community and faith-based groups across the country. It places thousands of young adults in positions where they learn valuable work skills, earn money for education, and develop an appreciation for citizenship. In its VISTA program, for example, AmeriCorps volunteers spend a year working full-time at fighting poverty. And through its partnership with the Federal Emergency Management Agency, young adults help communities recover from disasters. If you are eighteen or over and have the time, AmeriCorps is an excellent way to improve the economy of a community.

LEARN MORE ★ ★ ★

LOW WAGES MEAN TAXPAYER-SUPPORTED BENEFITS

In total, in each of the years of 2009 through 2011,

employers across the country received a subsidy of nearly $153 billion from American taxpayers for paying workers inadequate wages, according to a 2015 report from the UC Berkeley Center for Labor Research and Education.

The report and its background are at laborcenter .berkeley.edu/the-high-public-cost-of-low-wages.

$15 MINIMUM WAGE

Links to the 2015 Hart Research Associates memo and poll showing Americans' support for the higher wage can be found at: nelp.org/content/uploads/2015/03 /PR-Federal-Minimum-Wage-Poll-Jan-2015.pdf.

An up-to-date list of minimum wages by state is at: ncsl.org/research/labor-and-employment/state -minimum-wage-chart.aspx.

The History Channel has gathered short clips about labor history here: history.com/topics/labor/videos.

The Nation magazine published an excellent list of Top Ten Labor Day songs here: thenation.com/article /top-ten-labor-day-songs. The focus is on songs about working people and includes artists Woody Guthrie, Sweet Honey in the Rock, the Clash, and Dolly Parton.

TWO

REAL TAX REFORM

The tax code is helping the very rich get insanely richer, while the middle class is disappearing and the poor are getting poorer. We need real tax reform to address the growing income and wealth gaps.

PROGRESSIVE INCOME TAX

For the past forty years, Wall Street banks, large, profitable corporations, and the billionaire class have rigged the tax code to redistribute wealth and income to the richest and most powerful people in this country. At a time of massive wealth and income inequality, when major corporation after major corporation pays nothing in federal income taxes, and when many CEOs enjoy an effective tax rate that is lower than their secretaries', we need progressive income tax reform based on the ability to pay.

The problem is that way too much of the extraordinary wealth is owned by the top 1 percent, who, instead of paying their fair share in taxes, have been receiving huge tax breaks for years.

If we taxed the wealthy in a progressive manner, we could begin to address the most urgent needs facing our country. But we don't. According to Citizens for Tax Justice, the richest 1 percent of Americans, who took in an astounding 21.6 percent of all income in the

ACCORDING TO CITIZENS FOR TAX JUSTICE, THE RICHEST 1 PERCENT OF AMERICANS, WHO TOOK IN 21.6 PERCENT OF ALL INCOME IN THE UNITED STATES LAST YEAR, PAID JUST 23.6 PERCENT OF ALL FEDERAL, STATE, AND LOCAL TAXES.

United States last year, paid just 23.6 percent of all federal, state, and local taxes. That is not the kind of tax system we need in America.

It's not just the official tax rates that benefit the rich, it's also the loopholes. As Warren Buffett, the multi-billionaire investor, has often reminded us, he pays a lower effective tax rate than his own secretary. This is because capital gains (profits from the sale of a property or investment) and dividends (the money a company pays to its shareholders from its profits) are taxed at lower rates than wages and salaries.

And then there is the carried-interest loophole, a tax break that allows Wall Street hedge fund managers to treat most of their earnings as long-term capital gains instead of payments for services rendered. Although it makes no rational sense, this loophole cuts the tax rate in half for a small group of incredibly wealthy people—costing the U.S. Treasury as much as $180 billion over ten years.

In my view, we have to send a message to the billionaire class. We must close the loopholes and address the massive and growing inequality.

You shouldn't be able to get huge tax breaks while children in this country go hungry.

You shouldn't be able to continue getting tax breaks while shipping American jobs to China.

You shouldn't be able to hide your profits in the

Cayman Islands and other tax havens while there are massive unmet needs in every corner of this nation.

CORPORATE TAXES

Tax avoidance schemes used by corporations rob Americans of the revenue we need to provide basic government services, placing the financial burden on the backs of working families instead of profitable corporations.

★ ★ ★

The top corporate income tax rate of 35 percent is the third highest in the world, but most corporations don't pay anywhere close to that rate. A March 2016 Government Accountability Office study found that large corporations actually paid just 14 percent of their profits in federal income taxes from 2008 to 2012. Not 35 percent, but 14 percent.

One in every five large, profitable corporations paid no federal income taxes at all in 2012. Not 35 percent, but 0 percent.

According to a March 2016 article in *The Economist*, U.S. corporate profits are at near-record highs. It should come as no surprise that just as our tax code benefits wealthy individuals, it also benefits some of the largest and most profitable corporations in the world through tax breaks, deductions, credits, and tax avoidance loopholes. Our tax code essentially legalizes tax dodging for large corporations.

The Cayman Islands and Bermuda are two of the favorite countries for corporations to stash their cash, since they have secretive banking laws and no corporate taxes at all. None. All you need to do is set up a post office box in one of those countries, and voilà—you now have a foreign company, with no tax liabilities! The practice has become so absurd that a single five-story office building in the Cayman Islands is now the official legal "home" of about nineteen thousand corporations. Offshore tax schemes alone allow corporations to avoid paying more than $100 billion in U.S. taxes each and every year.

Offshore tax havens are nothing but legalized tax fraud and the fiscally responsible thing, and the just thing, to do is to eliminate them.

TWEET BY BERNIE SANDERS, APRIL 5, 2016, 6:19 AM

These companies benefit in innumerable ways from being based in America. They use taxpayer-funded infrastructure, access the most highly trained and productive workforce in the world, use numerous government services (and sometimes are awarded government grants and contracts), and so much more. They are proud to be American companies. That is, until it's time to pay their fair share of taxes.

Some of the worst offenders are the big Wall Street banks, pharmaceutical companies, and high-tech companies.

In 2015 alone, American corporations held nearly $2.5 trillion in profits in offshore tax havens, deferring payment of more than $700 billion in U.S. taxes. Seven hundred billion dollars. Imagine how that tax revenue could be put to use for Americans.

America is not broke. The very wealthy and huge, profitable corporations just aren't paying the taxes that, in the words of Supreme Court Justice Oliver Wendell Holmes Jr. more than a century ago, "are what we pay for a civilized society."

TOP TEN
CORPORATE TAX AVOIDERS

Here are some of the worst corporate tax dodgers in America. Not coincidentally, the chief executive officer of every company listed belongs to the Business

Roundtable—an organization that lobbies Congress to slash corporate taxes. But that's not all. The Roundtable also wants to raise the eligibility age for Social Security and Medicare to seventy, and to cut cost-of-living adjustments for seniors and disabled veterans. These CEOs callously promote the idea that increasing their corporate profits is more important than their fellow Americans receiving the benefits they have earned by working or by serving in the military.

JOHNSON CONTROLS

In November 2015, this manufacturer of auto parts and heating and ventilation equipment outsourced hundreds of good-paying jobs from Milwaukee to China, Mexico, and Slovakia. Three months later, the company—which ranks seventieth on the Fortune 500 list—announced it would acquire Tyco, based in Ireland, to save $150 million in taxes. It's not hard to understand why. Although Johnson Controls made a $1.56 billion profit in 2015, it not only paid no federal income taxes but also received a $477 million tax refund.

IBM

Big Blue has a long record of outsourcing good-paying jobs, slashing pensions, and cutting retiree health benefits. In 2015, IBM made nearly $6 billion in profits in the United States. Not only did IBM pay nothing in federal income taxes that year, it received a $321 million tax refund from the IRS, while also receiving $1.35 billion in government contracts. And from 2008 to 2015, IBM avoided $17.8 billion in U.S. taxes by operating subsidiaries in sixteen offshore tax havens.

XEROX

Xerox has established at least forty-nine subsidiaries in offshore tax havens, including nine in Bermuda, to avoid U.S. taxes. In 2015, it made a $552 million profit but received a tax refund of $23 million. In 2016, it eliminated over five thousand jobs.

AMERICAN AIRLINES

In 2016, American Airlines was ranked dead last in on-time flights, but when it comes to tax dodging, this airline is one of the best. In 2015, while making a profit of more than $4.6 billion, American Airlines received a tax refund of nearly $3 billion.

PACIFIC GAS & ELECTRIC

In 2016, this huge utility company was convicted of safety violations and obstructing a federal investigation into a gas pipeline explosion that killed eight people and destroyed thirty-eight homes. It received the maximum fine for these crimes, $3 million, which shouldn't be hard for PG&E to pay. While PG&E made a profit of $888 million in 2015, it received a $27 million tax refund.

BOEING

Since 1994, Boeing has shipped almost 60,000 jobs overseas. In 2014, shortly after forcing nonunion U.S. workers to accept an end to the company's defined-benefit pension plan, Boeing's CEO—who made $28.9 million in compensation that year—callously explained his decision to put off retirement: "The heart will still be beating, the employees will still be cowering, I'll be working hard." When it comes to avoiding taxes, no company works harder than Boeing. From 2001 through 2014, Boeing made $52.5 billion in U.S. profits, but received a net federal tax refund of $757 million and state tax refunds totaling $55 million.

GENERAL ELECTRIC

When it comes to dodging taxes, GE brings good things to life. From 2008 through 2013, while GE made nearly $34 billion in profits, it received tax refunds of nearly $3 billion. Meanwhile, during the financial crisis of 2008, GE received a $16 billion bailout from the Federal Reserve while its chief executive officer at the time was serving as a director of the New York Federal Reserve Bank.

CITIGROUP

The third-largest bank in America, with $1.8 trillion in assets, Citigroup needed a $476.2 billion bailout in 2008. When it returned to profitability in 2010, earning $10.6 billion, not only did it pay nothing in federal income taxes, it also received a tax refund of $249 million. A year later, it established 427 subsidiaries in offshore tax havens, including 90 in the Cayman Islands, to avoid paying $11.7 billion in taxes.

PFIZER

One of the largest and most lucrative prescription drug companies in America, Pfizer made $33 billion in profits worldwide from 2010 to 2012, but instead of owing federal income taxes, it also received $2.2 billion in tax refunds.

VERIZON

Not only did this telecommunications giant avoid paying federal income taxes on $42.5 billion in U.S. profits from 2008 through 2013, it also received a tax rebate of $732 million.

REFORMING THE PERSONAL INCOME TAX

If American justice means anything, it means ending tax breaks to the rich and powerful so that we can raise wages, reduce poverty, create millions of good-paying jobs, and rebuild the middle class. It also means implementing a fair and progressive tax code.

I propose raising taxes on American households making over $250,000, and individuals with incomes above $200,000. Under this plan, 97.9 percent of Americans would not see their taxes go up. However, within the top 2.1 percent, the rates would get progressively higher:

 37% on income between $250,000 and $500,000

 43% on income between $500,000 and $2 million

48% on income between $2 million and $10 million (in 2013, only 113,000 households, the top 0.08 percent, had income between $2 million and $10 million)

52% on income above $10 million (in 2013, only 13,000 households, just 0.01 percent of taxpayers, had income exceeding $10 million)

A PROGRESSIVE ESTATE TAX

Strengthening the estate tax is one of the fairest ways to reduce wealth inequality, while at the same time raising significant new revenues that the country needs to rebuild the middle class.

I propose restoring the minimum size of an estate subject to the tax from $5 million to $3.5 million, where it was in 2009. This would only impact the estates of the wealthiest 0.3 percent of Americans who inherit more than $3.5 million. And we should make it graduated to target the biggest estates:

45% for an estate valued between $3.5 million and $10 million

50% for an estate valued between $10 million and $50 million

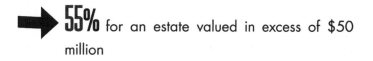 **55%** for an estate valued in excess of $50 million

There are all sorts of loopholes that help the wealthiest families avoid paying estate and gift taxes. We must close each and every one of them.

TREAT CAPITAL GAINS AND DIVIDENDS THE SAME AS WORK

Capital gains and corporate stock dividends are taxed at lower rates than the wages and salaries most of us live on.

The Congressional Budget Office estimated that 68 percent of this tax break went to the richest 1 percent of Americans in 2013. This is why someone like Warren Buffett, the third-wealthiest American, is able to pay an effective tax rate that is lower than his secretary's. To his credit, Buffett says this is profoundly wrong. We need to enact a real "Buffett rule" by repealing the low tax rates on capital gains and stock dividends for those who make more than $250,000 a year.

We should also repeal the exclusion of capital

gains on inheritances and gifts from taxable income. This exclusion in effect subsidizes wealthy families who hold on to assets to pass them on to the next generation, increasing the sort of dynastic wealth that is a feature of economic inequality.

A NEW TRADE POLICY

We have been losing millions of jobs as a direct result of our disastrous trade policies. This is a major contributor to the decline of the middle class, rising poverty, and the growing gap between the very rich and everyone else. We must do everything possible to stop companies from outsourcing American jobs. We need a new trade policy that encourages the creation of decent-paying jobs in America.

The reality is that during the last thirty-five years, so-called free trade policies have been unrelentingly bad for American workers. Written by corporate America, these rigged agreements have made it far easier for companies to shut down manufacturing plants in the United States, throw workers out on the street, and move to Mexico, China, and other countries where workers are paid a fraction of even the low wages that Americans earn.

Since 2001, nearly sixty thousand manufacturing plants in this country have been shut down and boarded up, and we have lost more than 4.8 million decent-paying manufacturing jobs. Not all these factories and jobs were lost due to our trade policies, but many of them were.

When we talk about unrestricted free trade, it is important to understand that these policies have been developed in a bipartisan manner, with the support of both Republican and Democratic presidents. Corporate America spoke, the leaders of both parties responded to its needs, and American workers suffered.

If corporate America wants us to buy their products, they damn well better start manufacturing them here in America.

TWEET BY BERNIE SANDERS, JULY 30, 2016, 6:49 PM

It is clear to me that the American people want their tax dollars used to put their fellow Americans back to work. They want government contracts going to American companies, not companies abroad. That's the way it's done in every other country, and there's no reason it can't be done that way here as well.

We must expand, not limit, "Buy American," "Buy Local," and other government policies that will increase jobs in the United States. This includes service-sector

REAL AVERAGE INCOME*

$8,000,000

$7,000,000

$6,000,000

$5,000,000

$4,000,000

$3,000,000

$2,000,000

$1,000,000

1980   1985   1990   1995

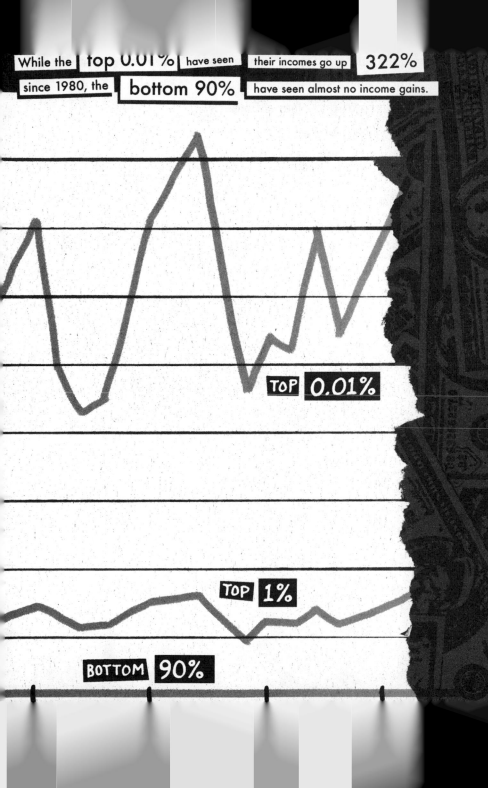

contracts that prevent companies from sending government call center and data processing facilities to the Philippines and other countries.

Moreover, we need to make sure that strong and binding labor, environmental, and human rights standards are written into all trade agreements. At a minimum, this means that all countries must comply with the standards of the International Labor Organization, multilateral environmental agreements, and the International Covenant on Civil and Political Rights.

We must add to every U.S. trade agreement enforceable rules against currency cheating, which allows countries to unfairly dump their products in this country and makes our exports more expensive abroad.

And we need to establish a simple rule that food may be imported into the United States only if it meets or exceeds U.S. standards with respect to safety, pesticide use, inspections, packaging, and labeling.

We must also take a hard look at the concept of applying a "social tariff" on imported goods. It is inherently unfair for American workers to have to compete against those in countries with abysmally low wages, minimal environmental standards, and poor records on human rights.

MOBILIZE ★ ★ ★

Citizens for Tax Justice (ctj.org) is a public-interest research and advocacy organization focusing on federal, state, and local tax policies and their impact on our nation. CTJ's mission is to give ordinary people a greater voice in the development of tax laws. Their blog posts and research papers provide in-depth tracking of tax reform—or lack thereof.

United for a Fair Economy (faireconomy.org) challenges the concentration of wealth and power that corrupts democracy, deepens the racial divide, and tears communities apart. They use popular economics education, training, and creative communications to support social movements working for a resilient, sustainable, and equitable economy. They organize groups at the state level to work for policy change.

Among many other initiatives, the Economic Policy Institute (epi.org) tracks the wage and employment policies coming from the White House, Congress, and the courts. Its research clearly defines the benefits to the economy of a $15-per-hour wage.

LEARN MORE ★ ★ ★

INCREASING TAXES ON THE WEALTHY

A June 2016 survey by the Brookings Institution and the Public Religion Research Institute found that almost 70 percent of Americans support increasing taxes on people earning $250,000 or more per year. The report focuses on many issues that shaped the 2016 presidential election. It is at: prri.org/research/prri-brookings-poll-immigration-economy-trade-terrorism-presidential-race/.

An April 2016 Gallup poll found 61 percent of Americans believe upper-income individuals pay too little in taxes. And despite conservative pundits who insist that redistributing wealth is fundamentally un-American, the American people respectfully disagree, with 52 percent believing that our government should "redistribute wealth by heavy taxes on the rich."

The Gallup poll on taxes is at: gallup.com/poll/190775/americans-say-upper-income-pay-little-taxes.aspx.

Watch Bernie Sanders's speech at the Democratic National Convention on July 25, 2016 here: youtube.com/watch?v=V0tVD87cZew.

REFORMING THE CORPORATE TAX CODE

Citizens for Tax Justice, ctj.org, is a public-interest group focusing on federal, state, and local tax policy. It uses research to advocate for making taxes fair for middle- and low-income people, closing corporate tax loopholes, and reducing the national debt.

FAMILY WEALTH TRENDS

A Congressional Budget Office report on family wealth in the United States is at: cbo.gov/publication/51846.

THREE

REFORMING

WALL STREET

Today, the ten major financial institutions in this country have more than $10 trillion in assets, equivalent to 60 percent of our entire gross domestic product. These banks issue more than two-thirds of all credit cards, underwrite more than 35 percent of all mortgages, hold 76 percent of all financial derivatives, and control more than 46 percent of all bank deposits. Meanwhile, their business model is based on fraud. It's time for real Wall Street reform.

REFORMING WALL STREET

The American people understand that there is something profoundly wrong when a handful of billionaires on Wall Street wield extraordinary power and influence over the political and economic life of our country. They understand that Congress does not regulate Wall Street—rather, it is Wall Street that regulates Congress.

Not a single industry in America has contributed more to congressional campaigns and political parties than the financial sector. None. Since the 1990s, the financial services industry has spent billions of dollars on lobbying and campaign contributions to get Congress to deregulate Wall Street, eliminate consumer protection laws, and repeal the Glass-Steagall Act that separated investment and commercial banking.

WALL STREET: MONEY
LAUNDERING, CURRENCY MANIPULATION, BRIBERY, CONSPIRACY, RATE TAMPERING, COLLUSION

It seems like every few weeks we read about a giant financial institution that has been fined or that has reached a settlement for its illegal behavior. Some people believe this is an aberration—that we have an honest financial system, but every now and then a major institution does something wrong and gets caught. Unfortunately, the overwhelming evidence suggests otherwise.

The reality is that fraud is the business model on Wall Street. And in the weak regulatory climate we now have, Wall Street likely gets away with a lot more illegal behavior than we even know about. Since 2009, major banks have been fined more than $200 billion for reckless, unfair, and deceptive activities.

Here are just a few examples:

JULY 2014 Citigroup reached a $7 billion settlement for misleading the public about the defective mortgages it bundled in securities. Then–attorney general Eric Holder said Citigroup's "misconduct was egregious . . . They contributed mightily to the financial crisis that devastated our economy in 2008. . . . As a result of their assurances that toxic financial products were sound, Citigroup was able to expand its market share and increase profits."

AUGUST 2014 Bank of America paid more than $16 billion to settle federal charges that it lied to investors about the riskiness of the mortgage-backed securities it sold during the run-up to the 2008 financial crisis.

FEBRUARY 2016 Morgan Stanley reached a $3.2 billion settlement with the Justice Department and several states for misleading investors about the quality of the mortgage bonds it was selling.

FEBRUARY 2016 The international bank HSBC agreed to pay $601 million to settle claims by federal and state agencies of abusive mortgage lending practices.

APRIL 2016 Goldman Sachs reached a $5 billion settlement for fraudulently marketing and selling subprime mortgage-backed securities, which were the foundation of the housing crisis. This is in addition to the $550 million Goldman paid to the Securities and Exchange Commission to settle a 2010 subprime mortgage lawsuit.

APRIL 2016 Wells Fargo reached a $1.2 billion settlement with the Department of Justice for "reckless" and "shoddy" underwriting on thousands of home loans from 2001 to 2008.

Money laundering, currency manipulation, bribery, conspiracy, rate tampering, collusion: these are the routine practices of Wall Street. And this is not just my opinion. This is what a number of financial executives themselves have acknowledged.

In a 2015 University of Notre Dame survey on ethics in the financial services industry, 51 percent of Wall Street executives thought it was likely that their competitors engaged in unethical or illegal activity to gain an edge. More than one-third had either witnessed or had firsthand knowledge of wrongdoing. Nearly one in five believed they had to engage in illegal or unethical activity to be successful. And a quarter had signed or been asked to sign confidentiality agreements that prohibited reporting illegal or unethical activities to the authorities.

When a trader from Barclays was caught trying to rig the $5 trillion-per-day currency market in 2010, he said blithely, "If you ain't cheating, you ain't trying."

And in 2006, just before the financial system began to collapse, an analyst from Standard & Poor's, a credit-rating agency that consistently and knowingly gave the highest ratings to near-worthless mortgage-backed securities, said in an internal e-mail, "Let's hope we are all wealthy and retired by the time this house of cards falters."

ENDING "TOO BIG TO JAIL"

Our country can no longer afford to tolerate the culture of fraud and corruption on Wall Street. The people responsible for illegal behavior must be held accountable. Unfortunately, that has not been the case so far.

Americans see that there are different rules for the rich and powerful than for everyone else. They see kids arrested and sometimes even jailed for possessing marijuana or for other minor crimes. But when it comes to Wall Street executives, whose illegal behavior hurts millions of Americans, they see that there are no arrests, no police records, and no jail time.

In 2013, I was stunned when our country's top law enforcement official suggested it might be difficult to prosecute executives of major financial institutions who commit crimes because doing so could destabilize the financial system of our country and the world. Since when did that

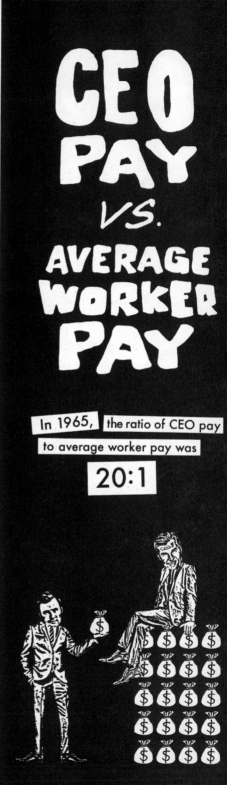

CEO PAY VS. AVERAGE WORKER PAY

In 1965, the ratio of CEO pay to average worker pay was

20:1

In 2014, it was

303:1

become a criterion for deciding whether or not to prosecute breakers of the law?

At the time, Attorney General Eric Holder told the Senate Judiciary Committee: "I am concerned that the size of some of these institutions becomes so large that it does become difficult for us to prosecute them when we are hit with indications that if we do prosecute—if we do bring a criminal charge—it will have a negative impact on the national economy, perhaps even the world economy."

There is something fundamentally wrong with our criminal justice system when not one major Wall Street executive has been prosecuted for causing the near collapse of our entire economy in 2008. That has to change. "Equal Justice Under Law" cannot just be words engraved over the doors of the Supreme Court. It must be the standard that applies to all Americans, including Wall Street executives.

FINANCIAL REFORM:
WHERE DO WE GO FROM HERE?

The time is long overdue for real financial reform in this country. It will not be easy, given the enormous power of Wall Street and its political supporters, but it is absolutely necessary if we are to have the kind of strong and stable economy that we need to rebuild the shrinking middle class.

We need to create a financial system that works for ordinary Americans, not just those on top. Here are just some of the steps forward that will help us achieve that goal:

★ To create an economy that works for all Americans and not just a handful of billionaires, we have to address the ever-increasing size of the megabanks.

★ We must end, once and for all, the scheme that is nothing more than a free insurance policy for Wall Street: "too big to fail."

★ We need a banking system that is part of a productive economy—making loans at affordable rates to small and medium-sized businesses— so we can create a growing economy with decent-paying jobs.

★ We need a banking system that encourages homeownership by offering affordable mort-gage products that are designed to work for both the lender and the borrower.

We need a banking system that is transparent and accountable and that adheres to the highest ethical standards as well as to the spirit and the letter of the law.

One might have thought that as part of the bailout, these huge banks would have been reduced in size to make certain that we never experience a recurrence of what happened in 2008. In fact, the very opposite occurred. Today, three of the four largest financial institutions—JPMorgan Chase, Bank of America, and Wells Fargo—are about 80 percent bigger than they were before we bailed them out.

If these banks were too big to fail in 2009, what would happen if any of them were to fail today? The taxpayers would be on the hook again, and almost certainly for more money than in the last bailout. We cannot allow that to happen.

No financial institution should be so large that its failure would cause catastrophic risk to millions of Americans or to our nation's economic well-being. No financial institution should have holdings so extensive that its failure would send the world economy into crisis. No financial institution should have such extensive economic and political power over this country.

If a bank is too big to fail, it is too big to exist. When it comes to Wall Street reform, that must be our bottom line.

REGULATING RISKY DERIVATIVES

We must also provide greater stability and transparency to the financial system by prohibiting taxpayer-insured banks from holding derivatives contracts on their balance sheets. Derivatives are the risky financial products that nearly destroyed the economy in 2008. They are basically insurance policies on future events that may or may not happen, like a corporate bankruptcy or a drop in oil prices or the collapse of the housing market.

Their value is based on the performance of the underlying asset, but as we saw during the financial crisis, the underlying assets are sometimes worthless. Yet that doesn't keep Wall Street from speculating on these complex financial instruments.

Today, commercial banks still have over $177.46 trillion of derivatives contracts on their books. That is insane. And I'm not alone in thinking that.

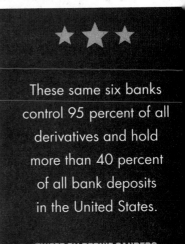

These same six banks control 95 percent of all derivatives and hold more than 40 percent of all bank deposits in the United States.

TWEET BY BERNIE SANDERS, AUGUST 12, 2015, 10:33 AM

As far back as 1992, Felix Rohatyn, the investment banker who helped New York City out of its financial crisis in the 1970s, described derivatives as the equivalent of "financial hydrogen bombs." The billionaire financier George Soros has said that his fund doesn't use derivatives much "because we don't really understand how they work." And five years before the 2008 Wall Street crash, Warren Buffett, the Oracle of Omaha, warned his investors that derivatives were "financial weapons of mass destruction, carrying dangers that, while now latent, are potentially lethal."

We must make sure derivatives that are held by investment banks, hedge funds, and private equity funds are strongly regulated. Right now, state insurance commissioners and gambling authorities are banned from regulating them. We must lift that ban. They should be treated and regulated like the high-stakes wagers they are.

All derivatives trading should be done in an open, transparent exchange similar to the stock market, without exceptions. As it stands now, these already complex and mysterious instruments are mostly traded in the shadows. It's time to bring them into the sunlight and see if they can withstand the scrutiny.

Financial regulators must ensure that all the participants in the derivatives market have enough capital to pay up if they lose their bets. Remember, derivatives are essentially insurance policies. Can you imagine paying for fire insurance on your house for twenty years, but when the house burns down, the insurer says it doesn't actually have any money to pay your claim? Without sufficient capital behind them, derivatives are the equivalent of selling an arsonist a fire insurance policy on your house. It makes no sense.

A TAX ON WALL STREET SPECULATION

As was brilliantly documented in Michael Lewis's book *Flash Boys*, Wall Street makes billions by buying huge quantities of stocks and bonds and then selling them shortly thereafter. The big investment houses and hedge funds have invested hundreds of millions of dollars in super-high-speed computers that detect the slightest price movements, then execute trades in mere fractions of a second. Once the price goes up—sometimes by just a fraction of a penny per share, and after just a few seconds or even less—the traders dump the securities. When repeated tens of millions of times, the practice reaps an unbelievably enormous profit for Wall Street.

Needless to say, this game of high-speed speculation adds absolutely nothing to a productive economy. What it does is make buying and selling securities more expensive for the vast majority of investors, including the administrators of American workers' pension and 401(k) funds. And, because it is largely computer driven, it adds yet another destabilizing force to the financial markets.

If we are serious about reforming our financial system, we have to establish a tax on Wall Street speculators. We have to discourage reckless gambling on Wall Street and encourage productive investments in a job-creating economy.

By imposing a small financial transaction tax of just 0.5 percent on stock trades (that's just 50 cents for every $100 worth of stock), a 0.1 percent fee on bonds, and a 0.005 percent fee on derivatives, we would tap the brakes on high-frequency speculative trading. And we would raise up to $300 billion a year, which I have proposed using to make public colleges and universities tuition-free. During the financial crisis, the middle class bailed out Wall Street. Now, it's Wall Street's turn to help the middle class.

REFORMING CREDIT-RATING AGENCIES

We cannot have a sound financial system if we are unable to trust the credit-rating agencies to accurately rate the creditworthiness of financial products. And the only way we can have that trust is to make sure that credit-rating agencies cannot make a profit from Wall Street.

Leading up to the Great Recession in the late 2000s, the major credit-rating agencies—Moody's, Standard & Poor's, and Fitch—would routinely give inflated AAA ratings to risky and sometimes worthless mortgage-backed securities and derivatives, even though the agencies knew the ratings were bogus. Without those AAA ratings, it is highly doubtful that many investors—again, including pension fund and 401(k) administrators—would have bought them.

The reason these risky financial

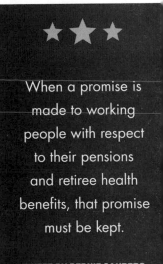

When a promise is made to working people with respect to their pensions and retiree health benefits, that promise must be kept.

TWEET BY BERNIE SANDERS, APRIL 28, 2017, 6:50 AM

schemes were given such favorable ratings is simple: Wall Street paid for them. Rather than providing useful risk information to investors (which is the reason they exist in the first place), the credit-rating agencies were colluding with Wall Street because that's where the money was.

The rating agencies' role in the Wall Street meltdown was extremely significant. By 2010, hundreds of billions of dollars' worth of supposedly AAA mortgage-backed securities had been downgraded to "junk" status—where they really were all along. But because they were purchased with inflated credit ratings that commanded a premium price, more than half a trillion dollars in value simply disappeared, almost overnight. And that was before a single house was foreclosed on.

Unfortunately, the ethical underpinnings and financial incentives within these agencies are fundamentally askew. When employees of Moody's were asked in an internal survey what their four highest job goals were, the top three were (1) generating more revenue, (2) increasing market share, and (3) fostering good relationships with customers. Fourth on the list was performing high-quality work. At least they were being honest.

In my view, we need to turn for-profit credit-rating agencies into transparent nonprofit institutions that are independent from Wall Street and accountable to a board of directors that represents the public interest. Wall Street must no longer be able to pick and choose which credit agency will rate their products.

ENDING USURY BY FINANCIAL INSTITUTIONS

Having a financial system that works for all Americans means stopping financial institutions from ripping us off by charging sky-high interest rates and outrageous fees.

It is unacceptable that people all over this country pay a $3, $4, or $5 fee each time they go to an ATM to get their own money. It is unconscionable that millions of Americans are paying credit card interest rates of 20 or 30 percent.

The Bible, and virtually every major religion on earth, has a term for this practice. It's called "usury." In *The Divine Comedy*, Dante reserved a special place in the seventh circle of hell for people who charged usurious interest rates. Today, we don't need the hellfire, the plains of burning sand, or the rivers of boiling blood, but we do need a national usury law that caps interest rates on credit cards and consumer loans at 15 percent.

Moreover, we must cap all ATM fees at $2. People should not have to pay a 10 percent fee for withdrawing

$40 of their own money. Big banks need to stop acting like loan sharks and start acting like responsible lenders.

ALLOW POST OFFICES TO OFFER BANKING SERVICES

Today, rather unbelievably, there are millions of Americans who live in communities that do not have regular banking services, where the giant banks don't think it's worth their time to invest. Well, what do you do if you live in such a neighborhood and need to cash a check? Where do you go?

★ ★ ★

We must also cap ATM fees at $2.00. People should not have to pay a 10 percent fee for withdrawing $40 of their own money out of an ATM.

TWEET BY BERNIE SANDERS, JANUARY 9, 2016, 5:16 PM

You go to a payday lender, who will likely charge an interest rate of over 300 percent and trap you in a vicious cycle of debt. You have to use the next paycheck to pay the interest, so you never catch up and get out of debt. That should not be allowed within the American financial system. We need to stop payday lenders from exploiting millions of Americans and making the poor even poorer.

Post offices exist in almost every community in our country. One way to provide decent banking opportunities in low-income communities is to allow the U.S. Postal Service to engage in basic banking services, such as offering savings accounts, cashing checks, and wiring money. The majority of postal services around the world allow their customers to do some banking, and we did, too, from 1911 to 1967.

REFORMING THE FEDERAL RESERVE

Lastly, we must fundamentally reform the Federal Reserve System to make it responsive to the needs of ordinary Americans and not just billionaires on Wall Street. The Federal Reserve includes twelve regional banks and a national Board of Governors.

When the financial system was on the verge of collapse, the Federal Reserve's board acted with a fierce sense of urgency, offering $16 trillion in virtually zero-interest loans to banks and corporations throughout the world. The Fed helped save Wall Street. However, it did little to save Main Street. And, as a result, millions of families saw their standard of living decline and their hopes for the future dim.

The decisions that the Federal Reserve made during the 2008 crisis sent a very clear message: while the rich and powerful are "too big to fail" and are worthy of an endless supply of cheap credit, ordinary Americans must fend for themselves. This was a clear case of socialism for the rich and rugged individualism for everyone else. But it doesn't need to be this way. The Fed was never supposed to be concerned just about Wall Street.

Americans deserve a central bank that works for them and not only for the big banks. We must reform the Fed to make sure it fulfills its full-employment mandate, increases wages, and rebuilds the middle class with the same sense of urgency that it showed when it saved Wall Street.

Let me outline how I believe we can do just that.

First, we must strengthen rules that prohibit commercial banks from gambling with the bank deposits of the American people. The Fed has to make it crystal clear to large financial institutions that the era of excessive speculation is over.

Second, the Fed must stop providing incentives for banks to keep money out of the economy. Since 2008, the Fed has been paying financial institutions interest on excess reserves parked at the central bank—reserves

THE FEDERAL RESERVE SYSTEM IS THE CENTRAL BANK OF THE UNITED STATES.

Formed to promote the effective operation of the U.S. economy and, more generally, the public interest, it works to:

★ conduct U.S. monetary policy to promote maximum employment, stable prices, and moderate long-term interest rates.

★ promote the stability of the financial system and minimize systemic risks.

★ promote the safety and soundness of individual financial institutions and monitor their impact on the system as a whole.

★ foster safety and efficiency in U.S.-dollar transactions through services to the banking industry and the U.S. government.

★ promote consumer protection and community development.

*Adapted from a publication of the Board of Governors of t

that have grown to an unprecedented $2.2 trillion. Instead of paying interest on these reserves, the Fed should charge banks a fee that the Small Business Administration could use to provide direct loans and loan guarantees to small businesses.

Third, as a condition of receiving financial assistance from the Fed, banks must increase lending to creditworthy small businesses and manufacturers to foster a job-creating, productive economy, reduce credit card interest rates and fees, and help underwater and struggling homeowners.

Fourth, we must eliminate the blatant conflicts of interest at the Fed. The reality is that the Federal Reserve has been hijacked by the very bankers it is in charge of regulating. Since the 2008 financial collapse, at least eighteen current and former Fed board members have been affiliated with banks and companies that received emergency loans from the Fed during the crisis.

Fifth, we must make the Federal Reserve more transparent. Too much of the Fed's business is conducted in secret, known only by the bankers on its various boards and committees. We must require the Government Accountability Office to conduct a full and independent audit of the Fed every year.

Currently, the Federal Open Market Committee does not release full and unredacted transcripts of its meetings to the public for five years. We must require

the committee to release those transcripts within six months. If we had made this reform in 2004, the American people would have been warned about the housing bubble well in advance of the financial crisis.

The bottom line is that we need a Federal Reserve that works for all Americans, not just the chief executive officers of large financial institutions.

MOBILIZE ★ ★ ★

EXPRESS YOUR VIEW

Many of the necessary changes in our economic structures and rules will be made at the national level, including efforts to reform Wall Street. Your elected officials need to know what your position is on bills brought before Congress. You should know how to contact your representatives and senators. Their staff keep records of opinion messages they receive from constituents. Take the time to become familiar with bills and express your informed opinion.

★ A list of senators and representatives is at congress .gov/members.

★ A searchable complete list of bills and resolutions before Congress is at govtrack.us/congress/bills.

★ Call your members of Congress. Dial 202-224-3121. Press 1 for the Senate. Press 2 for the House. Then say your state name or enter your zip code. You will be connected directly to the office of your senator or representative.

LEARN MORE ★ ★ ★

ETHICS IN THE FINANCIAL INDUSTRY

The University of Notre Dame survey in ethics in the financial services industry can be downloaded from the site: secwhistlebloweradvocate.com/pdf/Labaton -2015-Survey-report_12.pdf

The report, *The Street, the Bull and the Crisis*, was cosponsored by Labaton Sucharow, a law firm that specializes in corporate financial litigation and represents Security and Exchange Commission whistleblowers.

There are more than 150 TED talks about the economy. You can find them at ted.com/topics/economics.

Listen to William Cohen, author of *Why Wall Street Matters*, discuss how Wall Street and investment banks really work, how they are (and aren't) regulated, and what can be done to make them work better for everyone: wnyc.org/story/can-wall-street-work-everyone/.

★ FOUR
HEALTH CARE
FOR ALL

IT IS A RIGHT

Health care is a right. The United States must join the rest of the industrialized world and guarantee health care to every man, woman, and child through a national Medicare for All single-payer system.

A single-payer system is one in which a single public or quasi-public agency organizes health care financing, but the delivery of care remains largely in private hands.

It has never made sense to me that the quality of care people receive—indeed, whether they receive any care—is dependent upon the company they work for or the wealth of their family. Health care should be a right, not a perk of being employed.

It has never made sense to me that Americans are forced into bankruptcy because of a serious illness. In a 2016 survey by the Kaiser Family Foundation and the *New York Times*, 20 percent of working-age people with insurance reported having trouble paying health care bills, while 53 percent of people without insurance reported the same situation.

It has never made sense to me that some people live and some people die because of their health insurance status.

Most important, it has never made sense to me that our health care system is primarily designed to make huge profits for multibillion-dollar insurance companies, drug companies, hospitals, and medical equipment suppliers. The goal of a sane health care system should be to keep people well, not to make stockholders rich.

The idea of universal health care is not particularly radical. Canada guarantees health care for all its citizens through a single-payer system, and has done so for the past thirty years under governments having very different ideologies. In fact, universal health care exists in every major country on earth except the United

States. The details of the national health systems vary in each of these countries, but all of them guarantee health care for all their citizens, and none of them allow private health insurance companies to profit off human illness.

In America, even if you're "covered," it doesn't necessarily mean that you will get the health care you need. Despite the gains seen with the Affordable Care Act, which I strongly supported, the health care situation in the United States remains dire. Over fifteen million Americans lack any health insurance, and some thirty million are underinsured because of high deductibles and copayments.

DEDUCTIBLE: the amount of money a person must first pay out of pocket before insurance starts covering any costs

COPAYMENT: money insured people must pay as part of their care, usually as a set amount for each doctor's visit, procedure, or prescription

I have talked to people throughout the country who according to official statistics are "insured," but it doesn't do them any good. They still can't afford to go to the doctor because their deductibles and copayments are prohibitively high.

IN A 2016 SURVEY BY THE KAISER FAMILY FOUNDATION AND *THE NEW YORK TIMES*, **20%** OF WORKING-AGE PEOPLE WITH INSURANCE REPORTED HAVING TROUBLE PAYING HEALTH CARE BILLS, WHILE **53%** OF PEOPLE WITHOUT INSURANCE REPORTED THE SAME SITUATION.

I have talked to seniors who cut their prescription drug pills in half because they can't afford the outrageously high cost of their medicine.

It is not talked about much, but thousands of people die each year in our country because they can't get to the doctor when they should, or their care is cut off once they run out of money or are laid off and lose coverage.

Further, there are millions of Americans with decent insurance coverage who can't find a primary care practicioner because many regions of the country are medically underserved. There's a dire shortage of doctors in rural areas of our country. Some people who live there simply delay treatment and get sicker. Others die.

Most, however, go to the emergency room at the nearest hospital. This is enormously expensive. An emergency room visit is the most expensive route to care in the country.

A sane and efficient health care system should invest in the provision of health care and disease prevention services. We should be spending money on doctors, nurses, mental health specialists, dentists, nurse-practitioners, social workers, and other personnel who provide real services to people and improve their lives. We should be investing in the research and development of new drugs and technologies that can cure disease and alleviate pain.

We should not be wasting hundreds of billions of dollars a year on profiteering. Think about the many billions of dollars drug companies spend each year on television advertising that tells us what drugs we need to buy, and about the money they spend trying to influence doctors to use their particular brands.

We should not be wasting money on outrageous administrative costs. Think about all the people working in hospitals throughout the country who are not treating patients or improving their lives, but rather billing them and in some cases hounding people for overdue payments.

This waste and bureaucracy not only affect patients and their relationships with insurance companies and hospitals, but also does incredible damage to health care professionals. The vast majority of health care professionals in this country are people who joined the healing professions because they wanted to care for people, wanted to make a difference in the lives of their neighbors and others in their community. They did not want careers where they would be forced to spend countless hours in front of computer screens filling out forms, or on the phone arguing with insurance companies on behalf of patients. Health care providers today spend less and less time treating their patients, and more and more time justifying what they do and fighting to be paid by insurance companies for the services they render. As a result of this bureaucracy and insurance company interference, too many doctors and other medical professionals are simply refusing to accept insurance or giving up on the profession they love.

The irrationality of the current system can be seen most significantly in the huge amounts of waste and inefficiency inherent in this enormously complicated system. The United States has thousands of different health insurance plans, all of which set different reimbursement rates for providers and procedures. This results in extremely high administrative costs. According to a recent report drafted by thirty-nine physicians from Physicians for a National Health Program and endorsed by some twenty-five hundred medical doctors, a movement to "a single-payer system would trim administration, reduce incentives to over-treat, lower drug prices, minimize wasteful investments in redundant facilities, and eliminate almost all marketing and investor profits. These measures would yield the substantial savings needed to fund universal care and new investments in currently under-funded services and public health activities—without any net increase in national health spending."

In other words, eliminating the hundreds of billions of dollars now spent on wasteful and unnecessary administrative costs would free up all the funds we need to provide health care to every American. We don't need to spend more money on health care. We need to spend our health care dollars efficiently.

Our dysfunctional health care system impacts not only patients and medical professionals, but our entire economy. Given that employer-based insurance is the way most Americans get their coverage, small- and medium-sized businesses are forced to spend an enormous amount of time and energy determining how they can get the most cost-effective coverage for their employees. It is not

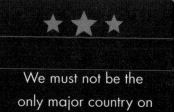

We must not be the only major country on earth not to guarantee health care for all.

TWEET BY BERNIE SANDERS, APRIL 13, 2017, 11:42 AM

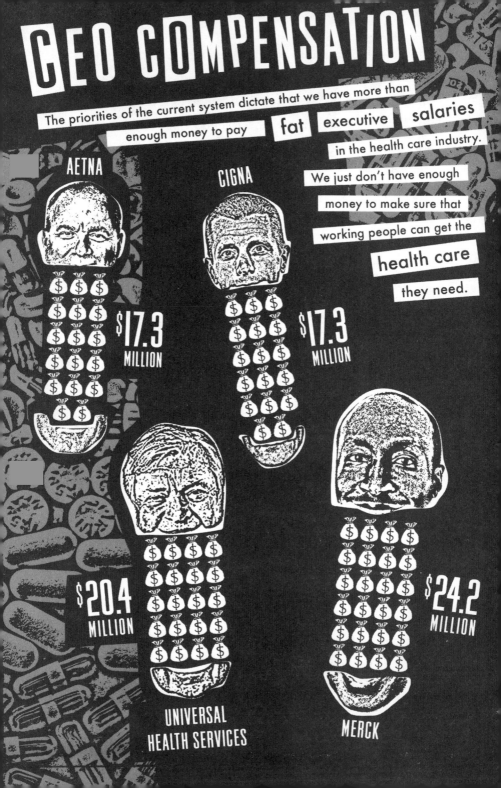

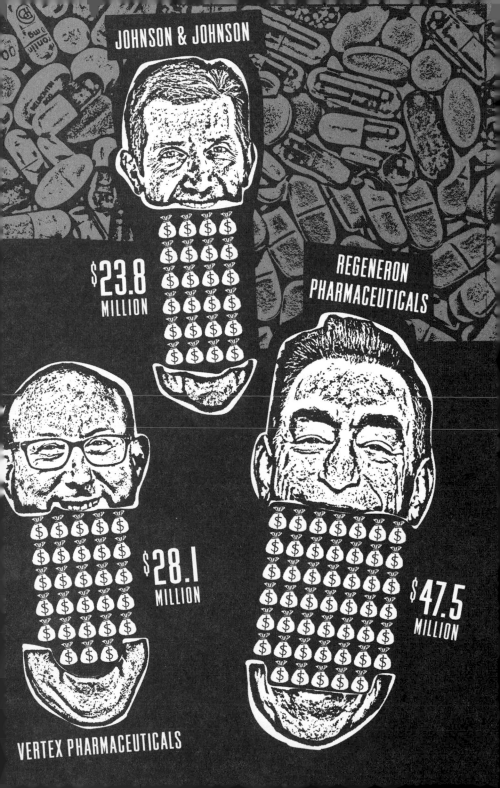

JOHNSON & JOHNSON

$23.8 MILLION

REGENERON PHARMACEUTICALS

$28.1 MILLION

$47.5 MILLION

VERTEX PHARMACEUTICALS

uncommon for employers to spend weeks every year negotiating with insurance companies, and many switch carriers every year or two to get the best deal they can.

When we talk about our current health care system, what is often overlooked is the negative impact it has on our entrepreneurial spirit. Millions of Americans remain in their jobs today not because they want to be there, not because they enjoy their work, but because their current employer provides decent health care benefits for them and their family.

Think about the extraordinary impact it would have on our economy if all Americans had the freedom to follow their dreams and not worry about whether the family had health insurance. Universal health care would provide a major boon to our economy, unleashing the entrepreneurial spirit of millions of people.

While health care costs soar and millions of Americans are unable to afford health insurance or prescription drugs, the health care industry reaps huge profits and gives its CEOs outrageously high compensation packages.

The priorities of the current system dictate that there is more than enough money to pay fat executive salaries in the health care industry. We just don't have enough money to make sure that working people can get the health care they need.

PRESCRIPTION DRUGS

When we talk about the high cost of health care in the United States and the inability of so many people to secure the care they need, we cannot ignore the crisis of outrageously expensive prescription drugs. In America, people get much sicker than they should, and sometimes die, because they cannot afford the medicine that they need. Sometimes the cost of their medicine is so high that they end up lacking the money to fulfill other basic needs.

Today in the United States, we pay by far the highest prices in the world for prescription drugs. A 2010 study showed that the United States paid, on average, double what Canada, Australia, and the United Kingdom do. A 2013 report from the International Federation of Health Plans listed comparative costs for the same drug sold in different countries. Here are a few examples of the different prices charged for widely used drugs in the United States and Canada. (In some instances, drug prices are even cheaper in other countries than they are in Canada.)

In Canada, Enbrel, a drug used to treat some autoimmune diseases, sold for $1,646, while in the United States it sold for $3,000. In Canada, Celebrex, an anti-inflammatory used to treat pain, sold for $51, while here it sold for $330. In Canada, Copaxone, a drug used to treat multiple sclerosis, sold for $1,400, while in the United States it sold for $3,900. In Canada, Nexium, used to treat acid reflux disease, sold for $30, while here it sold for $305. And on and on it goes.

While the five largest drug companies made a combined $50 billion in profits in 2014, one out of five Americans between the ages of nineteen and sixty-four was unable to fill the prescriptions their doctor wrote. So, people go to the doctor because they are sick; they get a diagnosis, but they can't afford the treatment. Then they get sicker. Does this make any sense?

One of the reasons the pharmaceutical industry makes huge profits is pretty simple. Unlike every other major country on earth, all of which negotiate prices with the pharmaceutical industry, here in the United States, drug companies can charge any price they want. And so they do. You can walk into your pharmacy tomorrow to get a refill of the same medicine that you have used for years, and the price could be double what it was when you got your last refill. And there is not a thing you can do about it.

One recent outrageous example of a greedy drug company is Mylan. For more than thirty years it has produced the EpiPen, a lifesaving injection that people with severe allergies carry with them in case they encounter an allergen. The drug cost less than $100 for two doses in 2007. Then the price began to climb. And in 2016, the company raised it by $100 to $608.61.

Congress and the states investigated the price hike and, in response, Mylan increased the number of people who qualified for their financial assistance program—usually in the form of coupons presented to drug stores—and began offering a generic version of the drug that sold for "only" $300. But the bottom line is that Mylan raised the price because it could. There was no law or regulation to prevent them from doing so.

Do you want to know why we pay the highest prices in the world for prescription drugs, and why there are no regulations preventing the drug companies from selling their products for any price they want?

It might have something to do with the fact that the pharmaceutical industry is one of the most politically powerful industries in the country, spending endless amounts of money on lobbying and campaign contributions. The pharmaceutical industry has spent more than $3.5 billion on lobbying since 1998. This is $1 billion more than the insurance industry, which was number two in lobbying expenditures.

LOBBY: to try to persuade a person, to try to influence the way the person will vote

The pharmaceutical industry, because of its great power, rarely loses legislative fights. It has effectively purchased the Congress, and there are Republican and Democratic leaders who support its every effort.

DENTAL CARE

When people talk about "health care," they are usually referring to the medical care we receive when we go to a doctor for a problem with our body. But health care is more than that. Largely ignored is the reality that we have a major dental crisis in this country. Tens of millions of Americans are unable to afford the dental care they need. They suffer with painful toothaches. They get teeth extracted because it's cheaper than getting the tooth properly treated. Without good teeth, people are unable to properly chew the food they eat, which can lead to digestive problems.

Bad teeth not only can cause pain and illness but also have an economic consequence. Try applying for a job when you don't want to smile because your front teeth are missing. Having bad or missing teeth makes it clear to the world that you are poor, which makes it harder for you to find employment, which perpetuates the cycle of poverty. And for kids, toothaches are one of the major causes of school absenteeism.

Throughout the year and across the country, doctors, dentists, and other medical personnel donate a few days of their time to treat the uninsured and underinsured at mobile clinics set up by a nonprofit called Remote Area Medical. People without insurance arrive early and sleep in their cars the night before the medical personnel arrive in order to make sure they get treated. We shouldn't have to rely on charity. The system must provide for everyone.

MENTAL HEALTH

And then there is the extraordinary crisis that we face in terms of mental health care.

In our country today, there are thousands of people who are suicidal or homicidal walking the streets, many of whom own guns.

In schools throughout this country, teachers find themselves increasingly overwhelmed with special-needs kids who disrupt their classes, and there is often very little help available. There is a massive shortage of pediatric psychiatrists and psychologists.

According to an excellent special report in *USA Today*, more than half a million Americans with serious mental illnesses are falling through the cracks of a system in tatters. The mentally ill who have nowhere to go and find little sympathy from those around them often land in emergency rooms and county jails, or on city streets. The lucky ones find homes with family. The unlucky ones show up in the morgue.

States looking to save money have pared away community mental health services designed to help people function, as well as the hospital care available to help them heal after a crisis. States have been reducing hospital beds for psychiatric patients because of insurance pressures as well as a desire to provide more care outside institutions.

> And while we don't guarantee health care to all, we do outspend all other countries on the planet on medical spending.
>
> **TWEET BY BERNIE SANDERS, MARCH 18, 2016, 2:36 PM**

The result is that all too often people with mental illness get no care at all. Nearly 40 percent of adults with a severe mental illness—such as schizophrenia or bipolar disorder—had received no treatment in the previous year, according to the 2012 National Survey on Drug Use and Health. Among adults with any mental illness, 60 percent were untreated. The time is long overdue for us to understand that a mental health problem should be treated like any other health-related issue. People must be able to get the mental health treatment they need when they need it.

HEALTH CARE OUTCOMES

Given that we spend far more per capita on health care than any other country on earth, one might expect our health care outcomes to be as good as or better than other countries'. Surely, with all the money we spend, we must be living longer and healthier lives, our infant mortality rates must be lower, and our people must be suffering fewer illnesses.

In reality, despite having the most expensive health care system, the United States overall ranks last among the eleven industrialized nations evaluated for a 2014 Commonwealth Fund report that compared health system quality, efficiency, access to care, equity, and healthy lives. The other countries were Australia, Canada, France, Germany, the Netherlands, New Zealand, Norway, Sweden, Switzerland, and the United Kingdom. America had the highest costs and lowest performance, spending $8,508 per person on health care in 2011. The United Kingdom, which ranked first overall, spent just $3,405.

Americans had the lowest life expectancy at age sixty of the countries studied, and the highest infant mortality rate. The prevalence of chronic disease also appeared to be higher here. In another study, the Commonwealth Fund found that 68 percent of U.S. adults age sixty-five or older had at least two chronic conditions. Compare that to 33 percent in the United Kingdom and 56 percent in Canada, and you can see the effects of our health care system.

A HEALTHY SOCIETY CREATES GOOD HEALTH

Let me conclude this chapter by stating that we must create a high-quality, universal health care system guaranteeing health care to all—but we must do even more than that. We must create a healthy society.

Most people understand that being in good health physically and emotionally is more than just a function of the care you receive—no matter how high quality that care may be.

If you are poor and struggling every day with the stresses of putting food on the table and a roof over your head, your health suffers. The life expectancy for poor people is much lower than it is for wealthy people, and there are parts of the country now where Americans can expect to die at a younger age than their parents did. This is often the result of economic despair and the resulting increases in drug addiction, alcoholism, and suicide.

If you go to work every day hating your job, there's no question that your frustration and anger will impact your health. People cannot spend forty or fifty hours a week doing something that they dislike without suffering serious health consequences.

If you are a senior citizen living alone and isolated, as many are, your health will suffer. Too many seniors in our country suffer from depression and alcohol-related problems. Friends, family, and community help us stay healthy.

If you are a child breathing filthy air from a coal-burning plant or some other source of pollution, your health will suffer. Clean air, clean water, and decent food are necessary if we are to stay healthy.

Everything is interconnected. Our political task is nothing less than the transformation of our nation. Health care for all, absolutely. But to create a healthy society, we also need to end poverty and provide decent-paying jobs for all people. We need a strong educational system, a clean environment, and equal opportunity for everyone regardless of their race, gender, sexual orientation, gender identity, or nationality. These, in fact, are all health-related issues.

MOBILIZE ★ ★ ★

As access to health care lessens, organizations that provide free or low-cost care need support.

Planned Parenthood (plannedparenthood.org) supports health care centers that focus on women's and men's sexual and reproductive health, including information and support for people with sexual orientation and gender questions. It provides information and services for both traditional and emergency contraception, abortion, and pregnancy support, as well as testing for sexually transmitted diseases.

Consider donating food or time at a food bank.

LEARN MORE ★ ★ ★

The Agency for Healthcare Research and Quality publishes reports, fact sheets, and tool kits in English and Spanish on health issues of national concern, such as the increase in newborn and mother hospital stays and opioid-related hospitalization by state. Its infographics at ahrq.gov provide snapshots of health care concerns. Click on Research, then Data Resources, then Data Infographics to find them.

Watch a Canadian family doctor testify before a U.S. Senate subcommittee on a panel comparing the U.S. health care system with the Canadian single-payer system here: youtube.com/watch?v=iYOf6hXGx6M.

★FIVE

MAKING HIGHER EDUCATION

AFFORDABLE

THE WORLD IS CHANGING

In the twenty-first century, a public education system that goes from kindergarten through high school is no longer good enough. The world is changing, technology is changing, our economy is changing. If we are to succeed in the highly competitive global economy and have the best-educated workforce in the world, public colleges and universities must become tuition-free.

College affordability and student debt are in crisis.

Young people graduate from college with huge debts. They should be looking forward to building independent lives and careers, but they are weighed down by financial burdens. Graduation should mark a joyous new beginning, not the start of an anxiety-ridden, decades-long financial bind.

One of the truly remarkable aspects of my presidential campaign—and quite frankly, one that took me by surprise—was how much the campaign resonated with young people. These vibrant voters were concerned about many issues, but the issue that was so often uppermost in their minds was the ever-escalating cost of college and the scourge of student debt. Whether they were thinking about attending college, were currently enrolled, or had already graduated, they were deeply worried that they would be saddled with an unsustainable amount of debt for years to come. Unfortunately, they were right to worry.

Unlike other types of personal debt that have been decreasing in recent years, student debt has been steadily increasing. In all, 44 million people—current students, graduates, and those who left college before graduating—now owe more than $1.3 trillion in student loans. This is more than five times the amount of student debt in 2004, and more than all credit card and auto loan debt in the United States combined. And an increasing number of those 44 million people will carry their student debt throughout their entire lives.

The high cost of college and student debt affects not only those who are in school and their families but low-income and working-class families who are simply not able to send their kids to college. Today in America, hundreds of thousands of bright young people who have the desire and the ability to get a college education will not be able to do so because their families lack the money. This is a tragedy for those young people and their families, but it is also a tragedy for our nation. How many scientists, engineers, businesspeople, teachers, doctors, and nurses are we losing because higher education in this country is unaffordable for so many?

It is disastrous not just for the individuals affected but also for the future of our economy and our economic competitiveness. The United States used to lead the world in the percentage of people who graduated from college, which is one of the reasons that we have the strongest economy in the world. Today, that is no longer the case. We now rank fifteenth in the number of young people who will graduate from college, and we're falling further and further behind. Does anyone really not believe that this will have severe economic consequences for the future of our economy and our way of life?

I believe that higher education in America should be a right for all, not a privilege for the few. That means that everyone, regardless of their station in life, should be able to get all the education they want and need.

the PRICE isn't Right

The average cost of college— tuition, fees, room, and board— for a four-year institution has skyrocketed over the last forty years.

1976 | 1986 |

$10,000

$20,000

$16,760

$21,650

$30,000

AVERAGE COST PER YEAR*

$40,000

$50,000

$60,000

*Includes tuition, fees, room and board for a private four-year institution, controlled for inflation in 2016 dollars (College Board, Annual Survey of Colleges; NCES, IPEDS data).

for higher education

1996 | 2006 | 2016 |

$28,140

$36,060

$45,370

If every parent in this country, every teacher in this country, and every student in this country understand that if kids study hard and do well in school they will be able to go to college, regardless of their family's income, that will have a radical impact on primary and secondary education in the United States—and on the lives of millions of families. That's what we can accomplish by making public colleges and universities tuition-free and making certain that all Americans, no matter their economic status, have the opportunity for a higher education.

Education has always been—perhaps more than any other institution in our society—the great equalizer. Education, especially in a rapidly evolving economy, is how people qualify for better jobs and how they do well at them. It is the key to solving many of the serious problems of economic, racial, and gender inequality plaguing our society.

There was a time, forty or fifty years ago, when many people could graduate from high school and move right into a decent-paying job with good benefits. Strong unions offered apprenticeships, and a large manufacturing sector provided opportunities for those without an advanced degree. A couple with a sole breadwinner could buy a home, raise a family, and send their kids to college. That was the American dream. Those days are pretty much over. With the loss of some sixty thousand factories in the last fifteen years, and the decline of the trade union movement, it is harder and harder for workers to make it into the middle class.

Today, perhaps the most important pathway to the middle class runs through higher education. While not all middle-class jobs in today's economy require a college degree, an increasing number do. People need a higher education to make it into the middle class and successfully compete in a global economy.

While it is my view that all students in this country, regardless of income, have the right to a higher education if they have the ability and desire to obtain one, it is important to take a hard look at why the cost of college is rising so rapidly. And it is also important to point out that the reason the cost of higher education is increasing is not that colleges are spending any more per student. Other factors are driving the steep cost curve.

One of them is the increasing cost of health insurance for staff and faculty. The fact that we have the most expensive health care system in the world significantly impacts college costs, just as it does any large business. Another major cost driver is the proliferation of administrative positions at colleges and universities. Just between 1993 and 2009, administrative positions grew by more than 60 percent, more than ten times the growth rate of tenured professors, and at many times the salary. As higher education becomes more corporate-like and bureaucratic, more bureaucrats are needed to run them. Exactly how much do students benefit by having, in some cases, dozens of vice presidents of this or that, each earning hundreds of thousands of dollars or more? Not very much.

Another reason college educations are becoming so expensive is that colleges are increasingly being run as businesses competing for market share. To become more attractive to prospective students, colleges spend huge amounts of money on fancy student centers and dorms, state-of-the-art gyms and sports stadiums, and countless other campus amenities. While this trend is certainly more exaggerated at private schools, public colleges and universities are not immune to big spending on bells and whistles that drive up tuition while providing little or no academic benefit to students.

Further, the cost of college textbooks has risen tenfold since 1977. The average full-time university student in the United States now pays more

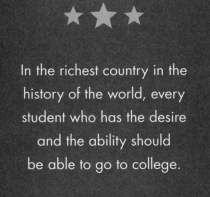

In the richest country in the history of the world, every student who has the desire and the ability should be able to go to college.

TWEET BY BERNIE SANDERS,
APRIL 13, 2017, 9:38 AM

than $1,200 each year just for books and supplies. This exorbitant increase is driven by stranglehold contracts with book publishers that restrict digital access to their products and release newer and more expensive editions every few years, which prevents students from using less-expensive used books. Let's call it what it is: a racket.

The high cost of college isn't just bad for students and their families, it's bad for our economy, too. While a college education will eventually pay off for many people, the large amount of debt incurred for that education has a real and immediate impact on the standard of living of millions, and on our national economy. Growing student debt is one of the major reasons why young people are delaying getting married and having kids, and why families are putting off buying homes, starting businesses, and saving for retirement. This, in turn, is slowing overall economic growth. And less growth means fewer jobs and less tax revenue to pay for the services Americans want and deserve.

You would think—for the sake of the overall economy, at least, if not for the students themselves—that government policy would allow people to get out from under unsustainable student debt by refinancing at lower interest rates. You would think that Americans carrying student debt would be able to refinance it like they can their home mortgages, right? Wrong.

Incredibly, most student debt in this country cannot be refinanced, even if the loan was originally made at a very high interest rate.

Unlike other forms of debt, student loans are very difficult to discharge, even in bankruptcy. In fact, it is much easier for a big bank or corporation to declare insolvency and be forgiven for outstanding debts than it is for an individual going through personal bankruptcy to be discharged from a student loan.

DISCHARGE A LOAN: to release a borrower from the obligation to pay a loan

So what happens if a borrower can't pay a student loan? Some borrowers have had their tax refunds withheld. Some student loans are sent to aggressive collection agencies that hound borrowers to the point of harassment. And some borrowers have even been arrested. America rightfully outlawed debtors' prisons in the mid-nineteenth century, but some cities and states are issuing contempt-of-court warrants that get around those rules.

Free college tuition is not a radical idea. In Finland, Denmark, Ireland, Iceland, Norway, Sweden, and Mexico, public colleges and universities are free. In Denmark, not only is college tuition-free, but people who go actually get paid. In Germany the public colleges are free not only for Germans, but also for international students, which is why every year more than 4,500 students from the United States enroll in German universities. For a token fee of around $200 per semester, an American student can earn a degree from one of the premier universities in Europe.

Governments in those countries understand the value of investing in their young people. They know that these students will acquire the knowledge and skills to strengthen their countries and become the teachers, architects, engineers, scientists, and entrepreneurs of the future. They realize that by allowing all qualified students—regardless of income—to achieve a higher education, they are making a down payment on their countries' economic prosperity.

CRACKING DOWN ON FOR-PROFIT SCHOOLS

Another problematic student loan practice is being perpetrated by the growing number of for-profit "career" schools that effectively see federal student aid as a profit center to exploit, without regard to the quality of the education they provide.

There is no question that some career colleges do a fine job of preparing students for employment in specialty fields. However, far too often these for-profit businesses lure students based on confusing or misleading information and exaggerated claims, and then charge excessive tuition and fees for poor-quality training in occupations that are either low-paying or offer few jobs. The now shuttered Trump University, which scammed thousands of people seeking to learn the inside secrets of real estate deals, is just the tip of the iceberg.

A college degree today is the equivalent of a high school degree 50 years ago. We need tuition-free public colleges.

TWEET BY BERNIE SANDERS, OCTOBER 26, 2015, 8:20 AM

The Senate Committee on Health, Education, Labor, and Pensions, of which I have long been a member, found that these for-profit schools spend, on average, about 30 percent more per student on marketing and recruiting than on actual instruction. It should not be surprising that students graduating from these for-profit schools have significantly lower rates of employment in their fields of study and higher rates of student loan default compared with their peers graduating from public and nonprofit schools.

But many of these schools don't care whether the

students fail after they graduate—their chief concern is making a profit off taxpayer-funded student loans.

The U.S. Department of Education has begun to crack down on the most egregious and predatory practices of for-profit schools. New federal regulations require career colleges to be much more transparent in their marketing and to make real efforts to improve employment outcomes for students, or else risk losing access to federal student aid. These "gainful employment" regulations, while not perfect, will increase accountability at for-profit career colleges and help students avoid becoming unreasonably burdened by student loan debt they cannot repay.

That's a good start, but we can and should go much further in terms of cracking down on these colleges that too often prey on students while making an outrageous profit off taxpayer money.

BETTER PREPARING
STUDENTS FOR THE FUTURE

We also have to better prepare students before they go to college by improving our primary and secondary schools, which too often are failing our youth, especially in low-income and minority communities.

Not everybody wants to go to college, and not

everybody needs to go to college. This country needs carpenters, plumbers, welders, bricklayers, ironworkers, mechanics, and many other professions that pay workers, especially those in unions, good wages for doing very important, skilled work. As part of a new approach to higher education and vocational training, we must provide those students with the education and training they need, regardless of the incomes of their families.

There are many other issues affecting primary and secondary education that are beyond the scope of this book. These include the effects of intergenerational poverty that disadvantage many low-income children, massive disinvestment in minority communities, lack of adequate after-school and summer programming, the opioid crisis that is ripping apart both urban and rural communities, and the chronic underfunding of schools. Suffice it to say that as a society, we are failing far too many of our children. These young people are the future of our country. To my mind, we have both a moral obligation and an economic imperative to do better.

MOBILIZE ★ ★ ★

Donate gently used or new clothing to Dress for Success, dressforsuccess.org. The organization helps empower women's economic independence by providing professional attire and support to women entering the workforce.

Join the movement to inspire young people everywhere to build the future we all imagine for them at the Future Project, thefutureproject.org.

Donate time to be a Big Brother or Big Sister (bbbs .org) through professionally supported, one-to-one mentor relationships with children.

Donate to, advocate for, or volunteer with Reach Out and Read (reachoutandread.org) and foster literacy by ensuring that young children have maximum exposure to books.

iMentor (imentor.org) pairs college-educated mentors with high school students from low-income communities for at least three years in its efforts to foster more first-generation college graduates.

★ SIX

COMBATING

CLIMATE CHANGE

YES, IT IS REAL

The vast majority of the scientific community agrees: climate change is real, it is caused by human activity, and it is already causing devastating harm here in the United States and all around the globe.

To my mind, global climate change is the single greatest threat facing the planet. It poses an actual existential threat to our country and our world. We are the custodians of the earth, and it would be a moral disgrace if we left to future generations a planet that was unhealthy, dangerous, and increasingly uninhabitable. We must transform our energy system and drastically reduce greenhouse gas emissions. There is no alternative.

Ever since the Industrial Revolution began more than two hundred years ago, we have been burning increasing amounts of carbon-based fossil fuels—principally oil, natural gas, and coal—to heat our factories and homes, generate electricity, and power our vehicles. And for most of that time, we have been dumping the by-products of that combustion, some of which are highly toxic, into our atmosphere, our soil, and our waterways. Over the years, we have become better at scrubbing out certain pollutants, including sulfur oxides and particulates that contribute to acid rain and smog, but an incontrovertible fact remains: when we burn carbon-based fossil fuels, we release significant amounts of carbon dioxide into the atmosphere. In fact, today, humans release between 35 billion and 40 billion tonnes of carbon dioxide into the atmosphere every year.

BY-PRODUCT: a secondary substance made in the production of something else

According to NASA scientists, in the past 650,000 years the concentration of carbon dioxide in the atmosphere has never exceeded 300 ppm (parts per million). At the beginning of the Industrial Revolution, carbon levels were about 280 ppm. Since then, atmospheric carbon dioxide levels have risen, slowly at first, but at an increasing rate as we burned more and more fossil fuels. According to the National Oceanic and Atmospheric Administration's Mauna Loa Observatory in Hawaii, the country's premier atmospheric research facility, the carbon dioxide level crossed the 400 ppm threshold for the first time in 2013 and continues to rise by an average of 2.6 ppm every year. So what does this mean?

Carbon dioxide is a "greenhouse gas" that traps heat from the sun and earth in the atmosphere. The more carbon dioxide in the atmosphere, the stronger the greenhouse effect, and the more the atmosphere and the oceans warm. This is hardly a new idea. Nor is it, as some would have you believe, a theory. In fact, scientists started connecting fuel emissions to the climate in the mid-1800s, and in 1917 Alexander Graham Bell used the now-popular term when he reasoned that with air pollution "we would gain some of the earth's heat which is normally radiated into space. . . . We would have a sort of greenhouse effect," turning the atmosphere into "a sort of hot-house."

And while carbon dioxide accounts for 81 percent of all U.S. greenhouse gas emissions, it is not the only problem. Methane, which is released during the

GREENHOUSE

As solar energy passes through the

Naturally occuring | greenhouse gases | only trap about
70% of the energy | and the rest is reflected back into space.

greenhouse gases

EFFECT

Earth's atmosphere, it warms the planet.

Increased levels of greenhouse gases, caused by human activities, trap more of that solar energy and warm the Earth's surface above the normal temperature, causing significant climate change.

increased levels of greenhouse gases

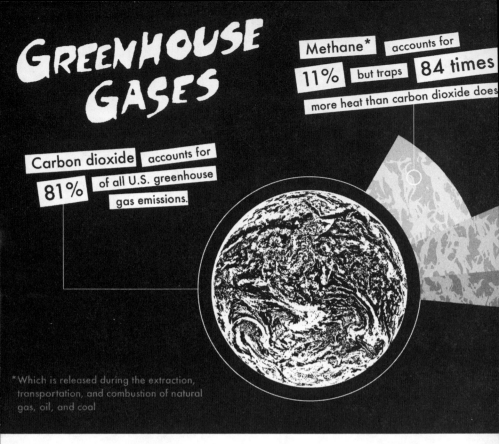

GREENHOUSE GASES

Methane* accounts for **11%** but traps **84 times** more heat than carbon dioxide does

Carbon dioxide accounts for **81%** of all U.S. greenhouse gas emissions.

*Which is released during the extraction, transportation, and combustion of natural gas, oil, and coal

extraction, transportation, and combustion of natural gas, oil, and coal, accounts for 11 percent of greenhouse gas emissions. But while it is a smaller slice of the overall greenhouse gas emissions pie, methane traps eighty-four times more heat, pound for pound over twenty years, than carbon dioxide does. Similarly, while nitrous oxide—also a by-product of fossil fuel combustion—accounts for just 6 percent of all greenhouse gas emission, it traps 289 times more heat than carbon dioxide. And certain synthetic fluorinated gases like hydrofluorocarbons and chlorofluorocarbons

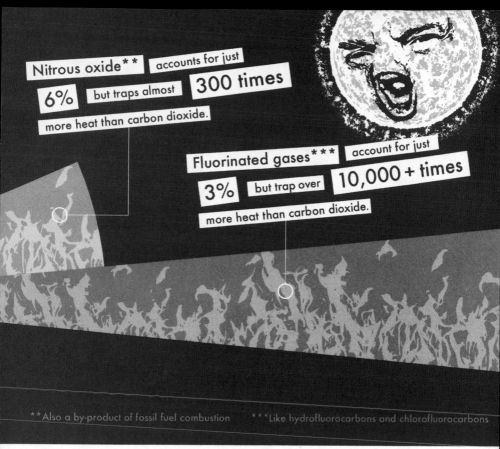

Nitrous oxide** accounts for just **6%** but traps almost **300 times** more heat than carbon dioxide.

Fluorinated gases*** account for just **3%** but trap over **10,000 + times** more heat than carbon dioxide.

**Also a by-product of fossil fuel combustion ***Like hydrofluorocarbons and chlorofluorocarbons

account for just 3 percent of the pie, but pound for pound, they trap tens of thousands of times more heat than carbon dioxide.

The results of dumping these heat-trapping gases into the atmosphere year after year are frighteningly clear. We are experiencing the hottest years on record. In 2016, July and August tied as the hottest months ever recorded on the planet. Sixteen of the seventeen hottest years have occurred since 2001.

Extreme heat waves have gripped large swaths of the planet, often with catastrophic results, especially for the elderly, the sick, and the poor. The deadliest heat wave ever recorded killed 72,210 people in Europe in 2003. A 2010 heat wave in Russia killed 55,700 people. In 2015, temperatures in India and Pakistan topped 117.7 degrees Fahrenheit and killed more than 3,477 people. In July 2016, the city of Basra, Iraq, reached 129 degrees—one of the highest temperatures ever recorded on the planet.

As temperatures rise, we're seeing significant shrinking of the ice sheets in Greenland and Antarctica. In Antarctica alone, NASA estimates that 118 billion tonnes of ice is permanently lost each year, which is equivalent to a quarter of all the water in massive Lake Erie. But that is nothing compared with Greenland, which is losing 281 billion tonnes of ice a year. Alaska and Canada are each losing another seventy-five billion tonnes a year from melting glaciers. Where is all the water from that melted ice going?

The oceans have already risen by about eight inches since the beginning of the twentieth century. That might not sound like much, but the National Oceanic and Atmospheric Administration predicts they could rise by as much as 6.6 feet by the end of this century. About 150 million Americans live along the coasts, and eleven of the world's fifteen largest cities are in coastal areas. An August 2016 report by the online real estate database company Zillow said that rising sea levels by 2100 could claim up to 1.9 million homes, worth a total of $882 billion.

Rising oceans are already creating the world's first "climate refugees." Residents of the Maldives, a tiny nation made up of more than a thousand islands southeast of India, are abandoning some of the lower-lying islands as the ocean rises. Closer to home, residents of Isle de Jean Charles in southeastern Louisiana, most of whom are Biloxi-Chitimacha-Choctaw Native Americans, are preparing to leave the only place they have ever called home as their land disappears. In August 2016, the six hundred Inupiat villagers of Shishmaref voted to relocate their four-hundred-year-old Native Alaskan village, one of thirty-one Alaskan villages facing an imminent threat of destruction from erosion and flooding caused by climate change, according to the Arctic Institute.

Meanwhile, the oceans themselves are warming and becoming more acidified as they absorb carbon dioxide from the atmosphere. These changes are disrupting important fisheries, threatening the food supply for about a billion people, and endangering fragile and important ecosystems like coral reefs, which are becoming bleached in the warm, acidic waters.

And all across the world, extreme weather disturbances are becoming more common, including hurricanes, torrential rainfalls, and severe flooding. In

October 2015, Hurricane Patricia became the most powerful tropical cyclone ever measured in the Western Hemisphere, with maximum sustained winds of 215 miles per hour and gusts up to 247 miles per hour. This was just a few years after Hurricane Sandy killed 186 people and caused more than $68 billion in damages and lost economic output. Sandy was such an intense storm that NOAA had to come up with a new term: "superstorm." And it is clear: warmer air means we can expect more superstorms.

The past five years have been the driest on record in California, forcing many towns to reduce water consumption by more than 30 percent. In 2015, more than half a million acres, or more than 5 percent of the state's agricultural land, was left uncultivated because of the drought, robbing the state of $1.8 billion in economic activity and more than ten thousand jobs. Historic wildfires scorched 118,000 acres of land last year, more than double the five-year average. Extreme heat has sent dozens of people, mostly in low-income communities without air-conditioning, to an early death. And along their 840-mile coastline, Californians watch cautiously as the ocean rises, threatening communities and businesses.

Meanwhile, there is another aspect to climate change that should concern us all. I believe that climate change is our nation's greatest national security threat. It is also the opinion of a growing number of leading national security experts, including many in the Central Intelligence Agency and the U.S. Department of Defense.

Of course, there is no shortage of national security concerns, including international terrorism, ISIS, global poverty, health pandemics, and the belligerent actions of countries like Russia, North Korea, and China. But unlike these other threats, climate change cannot be thwarted with good intelligence work or stopped at a border or negotiated with or contained by economic sanctions. It cannot be beaten on a battlefield or bombed from the air. It has no vaccine or treatment. And yet, unless we act boldly, and within this very short window of opportunity, it will likely wreak havoc and destabilize whole nations and regions, with serious security ramifications for many countries, including the United States.

The Intergovernmental Panel on Climate Change, which includes more than thirteen hundred scientists from around the world, says that unless we drastically change course in terms of greenhouse gas emissions, temperatures will continue to rise by as much as five or ten degrees Fahrenheit over the next century. Some scientists believe that number is on the low side. What will this mean?

What this significant temperature increase will mean is more drought, more crop failures, and more famine. Drinking water, already a precious commodity in many areas, will become even scarcer. Millions of people will be displaced by rising sea levels, extreme weather events, and flooding. Tropical diseases like malaria, dengue, and yellow fever will spread into parts of the world where they don't currently exist. All of this will likely lead to increased human suffering and death, but the situation will be even more dire.

The growing scarcity of basic human needs could well lead to perpetual warfare in regions around the world, as people fight over limited supplies of water, farmland, and other natural resources. A world in which we see mass migrations of people in search of food, water, and other basic needs is not going to be a safe or stable world. That's not just my opinion—that is the opinion of leading national security experts in our country and throughout the world. Yes, climate change is our nation's great national security threat.

And the sad truth is that the effects of climate change will fall especially hard upon the most vulnerable people in our country and throughout the world— the people who have the fewest resources to protect themselves and the fewest options when disaster strikes. According to the United Nations' Institute for Environment and Human Security and the International Organization for Migration, up to 200 million people could be displaced by 2050 as a result of droughts, floods, and sea-level rise brought on by climate change.

That is more than three times the total number of refugees in the world in 2016 who have fled for any reason, including dire poverty, war, and famine. Think about it. We have a major refugee crisis today. That crisis could become much, much worse in coming decades as a result of climate change.

I do not mean to paint a hopeless picture of a dystopian future over which we have no control, but Pope Francis was absolutely right when he said that the world is on a suicidal course with regard to climate change. Of course, we must not, we cannot, and we will not allow that to happen. We have to address this global crisis before it's too late.

DYSTOPIA: an imaginary place or state where everything is bad usually because of environmental disaster or total government control

While the global challenge of climate change is huge, there is no question in my mind that it can be addressed and effectively fought. There is also no question in my mind that the United States can and should lead the international

★ ★ ★

To me, family values mean leaving behind a planet that is livable for our children and grandchildren.

TWEET BY BERNIE SANDERS, APRIL 18, 2017, 7:57 AM

effort. As a nation, we have the knowledge and the technology, which is growing more effective and affordable every day. With millions of people in our country unemployed, we certainly have the manpower. What we lack now is the political will, in a failure to acknowledge the severity of the crisis and act accordingly.

Solar panels and wind turbines that deliver energy are a beginning. Municipalities are making use of methane gas that comes from old landfills, and many dairy farmers are converting cow manure to electricity. In Iowa, more than 30 percent of electricity is generated by wind turbines. In Texas, wind is producing some of the cheapest electricity in the country. In California, there are utility-scale solar facilities that supply electricity to hundreds of thousands of homes. The potential for energy production from geothermal, biomass, radiant energy, tidal power, and other technologies is almost boundless. We are making progress, but much, much more needs to be done. After all, the future of the planet is at stake.

One of the more profound lessons that I've learned in politics is that everything is related to everything else. Nothing exists in a vacuum. There is no clearer example of that than our failure to boldly address the crisis of climate change and how that relates to a corrupt political and campaign finance system.

On one hand, the scientists tell us that bold action

is needed to transform our energy system and prevent horrific damage to our planet. Further, poll after poll tells us that a significant majority of Americans believe we should be more aggressive in moving to improve energy efficiency and sustainable energy, not only to combat climate change, but also to improve our ability to provide clean air and clean water. One might think that in a rational and democratic society, when the people want something to happen and science tells them that they are right in wanting it, it would happen.

In today's world, that's not quite the way it works. In opposition to science and what the people want are enormously powerful forces who want to maintain the status quo. They are more interested in short-term profits for fossil fuel companies than in the future of the planet. They have a lot of power, they have a lot of money, and they know how to make a corrupt political and campaign finance system work for them.

In recent years the major energy companies have thrown unprecedented amounts of money at elected officials to buy their loyalty. Thanks to the disastrous Citizens United Supreme Court decision, the fossil fuel industry can pour unlimited amounts of money into the political system without having to disclose how much or to whom it was given.

Moreover, some in the fossil fuel industry have

intentionally lied about the impact of climate change and have funded organizations that have waged major campaigns of obfuscation and distortion. For many years the corporate media, especially television, heavily funded by fossil fuel ads, have either downplayed the significance of climate change or ignored the issue.

Excellent investigative journalism has recently revealed that Exxon did pioneering research on the effects of climate change in the 1970s and '80s, but Exxon executives kept the findings to themselves and later spread disinformation and confusion to protect its bottom line.

Charles and David Koch, extreme right-wing businessmen who have made most of their money in fossil fuels, have funded numerous "think tanks" to obfuscate the issue. According to Greenpeace, the Koch brothers have given over $100 million to climate-change-denial front groups that are working to delay policies and regulations aimed at stopping global warming.

All of this is eerily reminiscent of the fight over regulating tobacco, when representatives of the tobacco industry repeatedly testified before Congress that cigarettes don't cause cancer, emphysema, and other illnesses. As a result of their lies, how many millions of people throughout the world unnecessarily died? Over the years, how many trillions of dollars have been spent to treat tobacco-caused illnesses?

Our goal should be to cut U.S. carbon pollution by at least 40 percent by 2030 and 80 percent by 2050, compared with where we were in 1990. These are not unachievable, utopian goals. We can make it happen by dramatically increasing energy efficiency, aggressively moving away from fossil fuels, and deploying historic levels of new renewable energy sources like wind, solar, and geothermal. And we must help lead an international mobilization to make sure other countries make similar efforts. We can and must do this, for our children and our planet. Let me briefly address the steps we need to take to get there.

GEOTHERMAL: of or related to the internal heat of the earth

PROMOTING ENERGY EFFICIENCY

Energy efficiency is the low-hanging fruit in the battle against climate change. It is easy, it is relatively inexpensive, and every kilowatt we save through efficiency is one kilowatt that we do not have to produce. Pretty straightforward.

Forty percent of energy used in this country goes to heat, cool, and light buildings and run electricity through them. Making our homes, office buildings, schools, and factories more energy-efficient will reduce energy demand, save money on fuel bills, cut carbon emissions, and create good-paying jobs. We are talking about making sure every new building is built to the highest efficiency standards and that old buildings are retrofitted as much as possible to incorporate state-of-the-art insulation, efficient LED lighting, and modern heating and cooling systems.

It never ceases to amaze me that in my state of Vermont, where we still have some very cold winters, many people, particularly low-income families, live in poorly insulated homes. The reason is simple: they do not have the money to pay the up-front costs to weatherize their homes. This is an issue I have encountered over and over. The cost of an energy project—whether weatherizing a house, installing energy-efficient lighting, replacing an old heating system for a more efficient one, or installing solar panels—is often a barrier to implementing the project, even though these efficiency improvements can return as much as three or four dollars in savings for every dollar invested.

★ ★ ★

Renewable energy is our future—and people in Vermont and across the country are already working to transform our energy system.

TWEET BY BERNIE SANDERS, MARCH 19, 2017, 2:21 PM

That is why innovative financing programs, like on-bill financing and property-assessed clean energy loans, are so important for homeowners and business owners alike. These programs allow a utility or a municipality to lend customers money to make efficiency improvements. The consumers then pay off the loan directly on their utility or property tax bill while their energy costs decline. If this is not a win-win situation, I'm not sure what is. The barrier to up-front costs is removed, and the consumer uses less energy.

We must also take a hard look at increasing efficiency in the transportation sector, which produces 26 percent of all greenhouse gas emissions and half of all toxic emissions. New efficiency standards could reduce gasoline consumption by twelve billion barrels over ten years.

However, even then, the United States will lag behind the more aggressive efficiency standards in Japan, Canada, South Korea, and most European nations. Instead of the current goal of reaching 54.5 miles per gallon, we should, at the very least, set the goal at 65 mpg. If Europe can do it, so can we.

We must make hybrid cars and electric vehicles much more affordable. The potential reduction in carbon emissions from electric cars is enormous, especially as we transition to an electric grid powered increasingly by renewable energy. We should be funding cutting-edge electric car research—particularly advanced batteries—incentivizing the purchase of electric vehicles, and building the recharging infrastructure necessary for widespread adoption.

Lastly, increasing transportation efficiency means making major improvements to our intercity rail and public transit systems. Modern rail and transit systems would take significant numbers of trucks and cars off the roads, move people and cargo in a far more energy-efficient manner, and significantly reduce carbon emissions.

ENDING SUBSIDIES TO FOSSIL FUEL COMPANIES

The great irony of climate change is that American taxpayers are subsidizing the most profitable industry in history, whose products are quite literally killing us, to the tune of more than $20.5 billion every single year. For decades, we have given the oil, gas, and coal companies tax breaks, direct subsidies, and fantastically lucrative leases and royalty agreements to extract oil, gas, and coal from our public lands and off our shores. It makes absolutely no sense, and it has to stop.

It is an example of completely upside-down

priorities. For every dollar of taxpayer funds invested in renewable energy over the past fifteen years, fossil fuels have received eighty dollars! That is utterly absurd, especially when you consider that five of the largest oil companies—ExxonMobil, Shell, Chevron, BP, and ConocoPhillips—had combined profits of $93 billion in 2013, yet average an annual $2.4 billion in tax breaks.

The first step to weaning ourselves off fossil fuels is to end those huge subsidies, which energy companies have spent billions in lobbying costs and campaign contributions to preserve. That taxpayer money could be directed instead toward transitioning to a clean energy economy.

TAXING CARBON AND METHANE POLLUTION

Another important step in dramatically reducing greenhouse gas emissions is to start charging fossil fuel companies for the pollution they create. Quite simply, these companies make money hand over fist while taxpayers bear the costs of the harm to the environment and public health. We must flip that equation on its head and make energy companies pay for the true costs of burning fossil fuels by putting a price on carbon and methane. Not only is this fair, it would also be a game changer in terms of reducing greenhouse gas emissions.

In 2017, I introduced "100 by 50," legislation that sets targets for renewable energy production: 50 percent by 2030 and 100 percent by 2050. Technology has made the production of renewable energy affordable. We must stop climate erosion. This bill commits our country to doing so.

BANNING FRACKING

In the short term, we should put an end to the most environmentally horrendous methods of extracting fossil fuels, and to my mind, that begins with banning fracking. Hydraulic fracturing, or fracking, involves injecting a high-pressure mixture of water, sand, and chemicals into the ground to release otherwise inaccessible oil and natural gas deposits trapped deep in underground rock formations. While innovative from an engineering perspective, fracking is highly problematic for several reasons.

As was documented in Josh Fox's excellent film *Gasland*, the chemicals injected into the ground pose serious health and environmental risks to drinking water, air quality, and wildlife. However, the full extent of the risk is not known because the gas industry isn't required to disclose what chemicals are used or their quantities. If that complete lack of transparency sounds outrageous, it's because it is.

Moreover, the process of fracking leaks considerable amounts of methane into the atmosphere and groundwater—some studies suggest as much as 40 to 60 percent more than conventional natural gas drilling methods. And let us not forget, methane is eighty-four times more potent than carbon dioxide in terms of trapping heat.

Fracking is one of the main reasons I reject the notion that natural gas is a "bridge fuel" that can help us transition from oil and coal to clean sustainable energy. While it is true that natural gas burns cleaner than oil or coal, it still releases significant amounts of carbon dioxide when combusted. To my mind, being the best of three bad fossil fuel options does not make it a good option. Fracking simply increases the supply of and reliance on a fossil fuel that is contributing to global warming, while also doing irreparable damage to the areas where it is extracted. It's time to put an end to fracking.

LET'S JUST LEAVE IT IN THE GROUND

There are other extraction practices that should not be allowed, and there are environmentally sensitive areas that should be off-limits to exploration. Thankfully, the Obama administration banned oil extraction in the Arctic National Wildlife Refuge, which spans 19.6 million acres in Alaska and boasts the most biodiversity of any protected area north of the Arctic Circle.

We should also end all new federal leases for oil, gas, or coal extraction on public lands and waters. Public lands and waters are for the public to enjoy for generations to come—not for the oil companies to exploit for profit in the short term. This includes prohibiting offshore drilling in the Arctic and the Atlantic, entering into no new leases, and ending nonproducing leases for offshore drilling in the Pacific and Gulf of Mexico. If there is a lesson to be learned from the disastrous 2010 BP oil spill, it is that there is no such thing as safe offshore oil drilling.

We must also ban the practice of mountaintop removal in the Appalachian Mountains, where coal companies are blowing up entire mountaintops to get at the thin seams of coal below. The communities in the region are paying a huge price for this destructive practice in the quality of their health, culture, and environment. Let's invest in Appalachian communities to help them transition to a clean, prosperous, and healthy future.

NO MORE KEYSTONES

President Obama was right to kill the Keystone XL pipeline, but we must not let the present administration resurrect the project, or to ever allow anything else like it. The goal is to turn away from fossil fuels, and it would be very wrong to let a Canadian oil company pipe some of the dirtiest oil on the planet across the United States to the Gulf of Mexico. It astounds me that anyone could think that a pipeline transporting highly toxic tar sands oil near our rivers and fragile aquifers, particularly when it would then be exported to other countries, is somehow in the national interest.

INVESTING IN RENEWABLE ENERGY

Up to now, I have outlined various steps we need to take to move away from fossil fuels and dramatically lower the greenhouse gas emissions that cause global warming. We must concurrently make a massive and long-term investment in sustainable energy sources like wind, solar, and geothermal to make a seamless transition from dirty fossil fuels to a clean energy future.

One of the best ways to promote the development of renewable energy is to expand federal investment and tax incentives for building new energy-generation projects. The solar investment tax credit is an up-front credit equal to 30 percent of the cost of building a commercial or residential solar project, and the production tax credit is a 1.8-cent credit for every kilowatt-hour of energy generated by wind projects in their first ten years.

The solar credit is a huge reason why over the last decade, solar power has experienced an annual growth rate of nearly 60 percent and the cost of solar panels has been driven down by more than 60 percent between 2009 and 2016, according to the Solar Energy Industries Association.

Similarly, the production credit has made possible the development of wind farms that provided 31 percent of all new domestic power capacity in the last ten years. With proper federal support, it could generate 20 percent or more of our nation's electricity by 2030.

However, the uncertainty over the long-term prospects of these tax credits has stunted investment in clean energy projects, which often take five or more years to plan. Efforts to make the tax incentives permanent are met on Capitol Hill by that familiar refrain: we simply don't have the money. The hypocrisy of those who argue that solar and wind tax credits are too expensive or are no longer needed because the industries should be able to stand on their own is stunning. Taxpayers have been subsidizing fossil fuel companies through tax credits for more than one hundred years, and Congress long ago made those incentives permanent features of the federal tax code. And those who argue that renewable energy has hidden costs conveniently turn a blind eye to the fact that fossil fuels are cooking our planet—talk about hidden costs! It is time to end the hypocrisy and make the credits permanent.

CLIMATE JUSTICE

It is important to acknowledge that while the effects of climate change will touch us all, they will not be felt equally. As is so often the case, disenfranchised minority and poor communities will undoubtedly be hardest hit. Just take a look at the disproportionate impact of Hurricane Katrina on poor and African American neighborhoods in New Orleans. Do you really think a wealthier neighborhood would have had such substandard levees? Not likely. Which is why, as we develop plans to address climate resiliency, we must recognize the heightened public health risks faced by low-income and minority communities.

Of course, this is not a problem unique to the United States. In November 2015, the World Bank issued a report highlighting how the effects of global warming are already being disproportionately borne by poor communities around the world. That trend will only worsen because those communities are the least prepared to deal with such "climate shocks" as rising seas, extreme weather, and severe droughts. The report estimated that as many as 100 million people could be pushed into extreme poverty by 2030 because of disrupted agriculture and the spread of malaria and other diseases. This is why funding resiliency efforts in poor communities and mitigating the disproportionate effects of climate change on the most vulnerable must be a part of all international climate negotiations.

LEADING AT HOME AND ABROAD

Climate change is truly a global problem. The decisions individual countries, especially the advanced industrialized countries, make about their energy systems affect everyone else on this planet. The carbon dioxide released into the atmosphere in the United States, China, or Spain has no nationality and respects no borders, nor does the heat wave, hurricane, or drought caused by global warming. Moreover, even if the United States were to successfully transform its energy system to 100 percent renewables, it would not likely be enough to avoid the worst consequences of climate change. The fact of the matter is, we are all in the same boat together, and solving this unprecedented global challenge will require an unprecedented level of international cooperation. As the most powerful country in the history of the planet, the United States must lead that effort.

The December 2015 Paris Climate Conference was an important step in that direction in that, for the first time, 195 countries adopted a universal, legally binding global climate deal. But we all know that the fossil fuel industry has enormous power, and enormous influence over governmental decisions throughout the world. The United States can and should lead by example. Our country has contributed greatly to climate change, but we also have the largest stage and the greatest know-how to lead in implementing climate change solutions. Part of our challenge should be to show that the transition to a clean energy future can

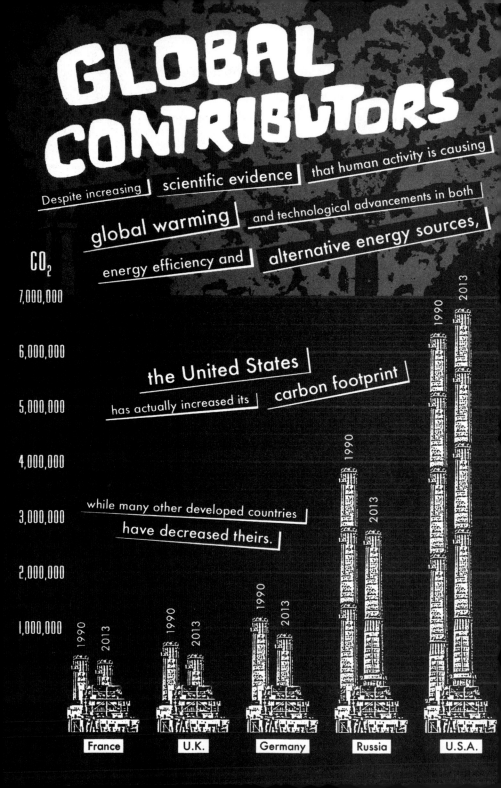

work, that we can produce affordable clean energy and strengthen our economy. Right now, the template developing countries have for industrialization is based on burning fossil fuels. With the largest economy in the world, we are uniquely positioned to demonstrate that there is a viable alternative.

Unless we take bold action to reverse climate change, our children, grandchildren, and great-grandchildren are going to look back on this period in history and ask a very simple question: Where were they? Why didn't the United States of America, the most powerful nation on earth, lead the international community in cutting greenhouse gas emissions and preventing the devastating damage that the scientific community was sure would come?

★ ★ ★

Our message is simple. We will fight to transform our energy system away from fossil fuel to sustainable energy.

TWEET BY BERNIE SANDERS, APRIL 29, 2017, 9:36 AM

MOBILIZE ★ ★ ★

Sign up for action alerts and support Earthjustice (earthjustice.org). Its tagline, "Because the earth needs a good lawyer," describes its work to hold accountable those who break environmental laws. The site provides information on initiatives such as the protests against the Dakota Access Pipeline.

Friends of the Earth (foe.org) is a network of seventy-five grassroots environmental groups around the world that take action on such issues as climate, food production, forest and wildland protection, and economic justice.

NextGen Climate (nextgenclimate.org) acts politically to prevent climate disaster. The site helps you contact Congress, offers petitions to sign, and provides links to news stories.

350.org is an international organization committed to decreasing carbon dioxide in the atmosphere. You can filter actions by region or topic on their website, 350 .org.

Greenpeace works to expose and find solutions for environmental problems around the world. Its website, greenpeace.org, lists hundreds of opportunities to volunteer and take action locally.

LEARN MORE ★ ★ ★

NASA publishes up-to-date vital signs of the planet, with full reports on carbon emissions, temperature, and ice and sea levels. Facts, articles, solutions, and resources are available at the excellent climate.nasa.gov.

The sad story of Shishmaref, Alaska, is told here: pmel .noaa.gov/arctic-zone/detect/human-shishmaref.shtml. The page includes links to sites maintained by indigenous peoples and to scientific studies on the disappearance of sea ice.

The 2006 documentary *An Inconvenient Truth* profiles former Vice President Al Gore's efforts to educate the public about the dangers of climate change.

There are more than seventy-five TED talks about climate change, including lectures by scientist James Hansen, Al Gore, and Mary Robinson, the former United Nations high commissioner for human rights, here: ted.com/topics/climate+change.

★ SEVEN

WE NEED REAL POLICING

& CRIMINAL JUSTICE REFORM

THE SAD REALITY

In the United States today we have more people in jail than any other country on earth. We are spending $80 billion a year to lock up 2.3 million Americans, disproportionately African American. To my mind, it makes a lot more sense to invest in education and jobs than in jails and incarceration. It's time for real criminal justice reform.

IN PRISON LOCKED UP

In the · United States · today we have · more people

PRISON POPULATION IN MILLIONS

1.6
1.4
1.2
1.0
.8
.6
.4
.2

1925 1935 1945 1955 1965 197

President Richard Nixon

declares a "War on Drugs"

1971

1925 1935 1945 1955 1965 1975

in jail | than any other country | on Earth.

1985   1995   2005   2015

1.5

1.3

1.1

0.9

0.7

UNITED STATES PRISONER POPULATION 1925–2015

1985

The sad reality is that racism has plagued the United States since before its founding. The atrocities committed against the Native Americans who inhabited this land long before Europeans arrived are beyond appalling, as is the abomination of slavery perpetrated against Africans brought to this continent to labor in servitude, as well as their descendants. Racism has affected people who immigrated to this country from Latin America and Asia. It has affected the Irish, the Italians, and the Jews. Racism has afflicted our nation for centuries, and it continues to afflict our nation today.

There is no question that in recent decades we have made significant progress in creating a country where we judge people not by the color of their skin, not by the language they speak, not by the country they came from, but, as Dr. Martin Luther King Jr. urged, by the content of their character and their qualities as human beings.

But make no mistake about it. While we have come a long way, there is still a long distance to go before we fulfill Dr. King's dream.

POLICE DEPARTMENT REFORM

Among many other struggles we must engage in to combat racism in this country, we must stop police brutality and the killing of unarmed African Americans. This has emerged as one of the great civil rights issues of the early twenty-first century.

The names and the incidents are all too familiar to us—innocent people who should be alive today, but who died after contact with the police. Sandra Bland, Michael Brown, Rekia Boyd, Eric Garner, Walter Scott, Freddie Gray, Jessica Hernandez, Tamir Rice, Jonathan Ferrell, Philando Castile, Alton Sterling, Oscar Grant, Antonio Zambrano-Montes, Laquan McDonald, Samuel DuBose, and Anastacio Hernandez-Rojas—and many others. We know their names. Each of them died at the hands of police officers or in police custody.

Eric Garner was choked to death in New York City after selling single cigarettes. Alton Sterling was shot while pinned on the ground by Baton Rouge police, who were called because Sterling was selling CDs outside a store. Freddie Gray died of a spinal cord injury while in Baltimore police custody. Twelve-year-old Tamir Rice was killed by Cleveland police

★ ★ ★

Violence and brutality, particularly at the hands of the police, are unacceptable and must not be tolerated.

TWEET BY BERNIE SANDERS, MARCH 25, 2016, 6:12 PM

officers within two seconds of their arrival on the scene.

Sandra Bland was ordered from her car, handcuffed, and thrown to the ground. Three days later, she was found dead in her Texas jail cell. Samuel DuBose was fatally shot in Cincinnati during a traffic stop for a missing front license plate. Philando Castile was killed by an officer in a Minneapolis suburb during a traffic stop for a busted taillight. Walter Scott was pulled over for a broken brake light in South Carolina and shot in the back by an officer. And on and on it goes.

Across the nation, too many African Americans and other minorities find themselves subjected to a system that treats citizens who have not committed crimes like criminals. Because of overpolicing in minority communities and racial profiling, African Americans are twice as likely to be arrested and three times as likely as whites to experience the use of force during encounters with the police. Although there is no national database of police shootings, one group that tracks these cases says that in 2015, police officers killed at least 102 unarmed black people, five times the rate at which they killed unarmed whites.

Violence and brutality of any kind at the hands of the police are unacceptable and must not be tolerated. It is no wonder that a growing number of communities of color do not trust the police.

Being a police officer is an extremely difficult and stressful job. Many officers are underpaid and under-trained and have irregular schedules that hurt their family lives. The vast majority of those who serve in law enforcement are decent, hardworking people who want to make their communities better places to live, and many have sacrificed much to do their jobs.

To my mind, that is all the more reason we must stand up and denounce acts of illegal behavior when they are perpetrated by the police. Police officers must be held accountable. In a society based on law, nobody can be above the law, especially those who are charged with enforcing it.

WE MUST END THE WAR ON DRUGS

Of course, the intersection of racism and criminal justice is not limited to police violence. An even bigger issue is the failed war on drugs, which has over the decades harmed millions through the arrest and jailing of people for nonviolent crimes. The number of incarcerated drug offenders has increased twelvefold since 1980, and this "war" has disproportionately targeted people of color.

According to the 2015 National Survey on Drug Use and Health, blacks and whites use drugs at roughly the same overall rates. However, blacks are arrested for drug use at far greater rates than whites, largely because of overpolicing, racial profiling, and—according to the Department of Justice—the fact that black motorists are three times more likely than whites to be searched during a traffic stop.

Take marijuana use. How many encounters between young people and the police begin with officers detecting the odor of marijuana? According to the best research, blacks smoke marijuana at a slightly higher rate than whites. According to the American Civil Liberties Union, however, blacks are four times more likely to be arrested for marijuana possession.

And marijuana is inexplicably a Schedule I drug—the designation for highly dangerous and addictive drugs such as heroin—under the federal Controlled Substances Act. Now, people can argue about the pros and cons of legalizing marijuana, just as we can argue the merits of the legality of tobacco, which causes cancer and other terrible diseases. But no sane person thinks that marijuana is equivalent to heroin, a killer drug, in terms of its health impact. But that is the way it's treated. To fully grasp how this affects our criminal justice system, consider that in 2014 there were 620,000 total marijuana possession arrests. That's more than one every minute. And that's a major reason why African Americans account for 37 percent of those arrested for drug offenses when they only comprise 14 percent of regular drug users.

Overall, blacks are imprisoned at seven times the rate of whites. In fact, according to recent statistics, one of every fifteen African American men is incarcerated, compared with one in every 106 white men. If current trends continue, one in four black males born today can expect to spend time in prison during his lifetime. This is the destruction of a generation. This must change. Sadly, the situation is not that much better for African American women, who are three times more likely than white women to be incarcerated.

Moreover, African Americans face more serious consequences when sentenced. Even when convicted for the exact same crimes, black offenders receive sentences that are on average 10 percent longer than those received by white offenders. These statistics, needless to say, raise serious doubts about equal treatment under the law. Just look at the outcomes: African Americans and Latinos together comprised 57 percent of all prisoners in 2015, even though neither of these two groups makes up even one-quarter of the U.S. population. Meanwhile, African American youth alone make up 40 percent of all confined youth today.

Further, what has to be understood is that, according to the Federal Bureau of Investigation, just 6 percent of African American arrests in 2015 were for violent crimes and another 14 percent were for property crimes. What is driving the incarceration of blacks is nonviolent drug-related crimes. In fact, according to the Federal Bureau of Prisons in January 2017, 46.4 percent of all federal prisoners are locked up for nonviolent drug offenses. This is expensive. It is a waste of human potential. We must end the over-incarceration of nonviolent young Americans who do not pose a serious threat to our society.

And if anyone thinks that a criminal record for marijuana is some small matter, think again. There are a lot of people out there who apply for jobs and don't get them because they have such a record. There are real consequences.

ADDRESSING THE MENTAL HEALTH CRISIS

The time is long overdue for this country to understand that we cannot jail our way out of health problems like mental illness and drug addiction. Our country is facing an opioid crisis, both in terms of prescription pain medicine abuse and heroin addiction. People are dying every day from overdoses. But the solution is not to lock up addicts. We have to treat substance abuse as what

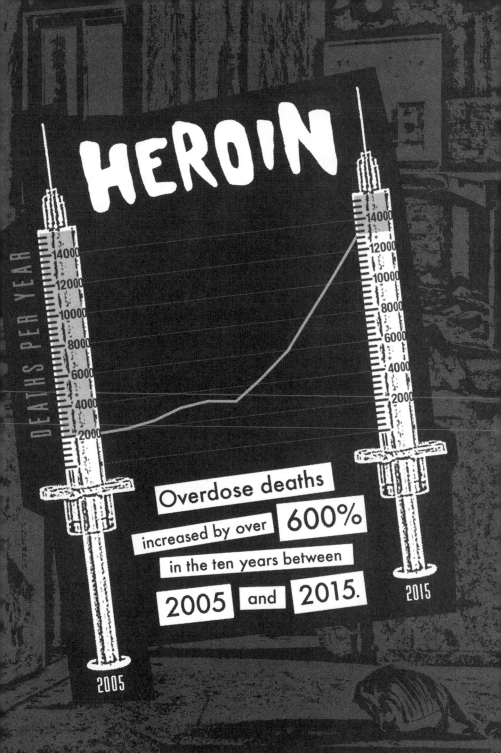

Source: National Center for Health Statistics, CDC Wonder

it is—a serious public health issue rather than a criminal issue—so that all people, regardless of their income, can get the help they need.

In terms of treating addiction, we put far too little emphasis on coordinated treatment and support programs that combine medication-assisted therapies, such as methadone and buprenorphine, with counseling and behavioral therapies.

We must also understand that we have a mental health crisis in this country and that many mentally ill people are ending up in jail because there is no place else for them to go. Over the last several decades we have made a bad situation even worse by cutting back on the programs and support systems that mentally ill people need in order to survive and improve. Of the more than 43 million adults with a mental illness, fewer than half received the mental health services they needed in the past year. We think we're saving money by cutting back on housing and treatment for the mentally ill, but we spend far, far more when vulnerable people end up in jail.

The end result of the war on drugs and our failure to treat mental illness in a rational way is that the United States of America has more people in jails and prisons than any other country on earth. We have around 4 percent of the world's population, yet we have more than 20 percent of all prisoners. We now have more people in jails and prisons than does the communist totalitarian state of China, which has a population four times our own.

It is a national tragedy that the number of incarcerated Americans has more than quadrupled since Ronald Reagan first ran on a "get tough on crime" platform—from about 500,000 in 1980 to more than 2.3 million today. And we spend $80 billion a year in federal, state, and local taxpayer dollars to lock them up. Eighty billion dollars a year! I can think of an awful lot of real needs that can be met with $80 billion a year.

ENDING PRIVATE PRISONS

Private corporations should not be making profits off of the incarceration of human beings. But that is exactly what is happening today in our country. According to the ACLU, as part of the movement toward privatization that we are seeing in sector after sector, the number of adult prisoners housed in private prisons has jumped almost 1,600 percent between 1990 and 2009. In 2015, there were about 126,000 federal and state prisoners in private facilities.

According to a February 2016 report by In the Public Interest, the two largest private prison operators in the United States made a combined $361 million housing these prisoners. The Corrections Corporation of America, the nation's largest private prison operator, collected $3,356 in profit per prisoner, while GEO Group, the country's second largest, made $2,135 in profit per prisoner. And yet, study after study has shown that private prisons are not cheaper, they're not safer, and they do not provide better outcomes for either the prisoners or the state. What they do provide is an incentive to keep prison beds full. They interfere with the administration of justice. No one, in my view, should be allowed to profit from putting more people behind bars.

The private prison racket extends to the Department of Homeland Security, too. More than 60 percent of all immigration detention beds are in prisons operated by for-profit corporations. These include two of the country's three family detention centers that house unaccompanied minors and mothers with babies, where there have been reports of inadequate food and medical treatment, sexual abuse, and other serious human rights abuses.

ENDING THE DEATH PENALTY

It is long past time for the United States of America to join almost every other advanced country on earth in abolishing the death penalty. The death penalty is cruel and unusual punishment. It is applied disproportionately to people of color. It has been proven to not deter violent crime. The inevitable endless judicial appeals tie up the courts for years at the taxpayer's expense. And far too many of those executed by the states are now thought to have been innocent.

We are all shocked and disgusted by some of the horrific murders that we see in this country. When people commit horrendous crimes, we should lock them up and throw away the key. But the state, in a democratic and civilized society, should not itself be involved in murder.

Frankly, we should not be in the company of China (the world's leader in use of the death penalty), Saudi Arabia, Iran, Iraq, Sudan, Yemen, Egypt, and Somalia. Rather, we should be in the company of virtually every other major democratic society that understands that even when confronted with unspeakable violence, we must move beyond ancient concepts of revenge. We must recognize, as Mohandas Gandhi did, that in the end an "eye for an eye" simply makes everybody blind.

ENDING THE SCHOOL-TO-JAIL PIPELINE

In this country, we treat our children shamefully. We have one of the highest rates of childhood poverty among the major countries on earth, and we maintain a dysfunctional child-care system. But as bad as the situation is for kids in our country as a whole, it is far worse in minority communities.

Black children make up just 18 percent of preschool enrollees, but 48 percent of the preschoolers who received multiple out-of-school suspensions. We are failing our black children before they even start kindergarten. Even though we know that 90 percent of brain development occurs between birth and five years of age, we allow early-childhood education in minority communities to remain a total disgrace.

Black elementary and high school students are more than four times as likely as whites to attend schools where more than 20 percent of the teachers are not certified. They are more likely to attend schools with higher concentrations of first-year teachers. They are suspended or expelled at three times the rate of white students. According to the Department of Education, African American students are more likely to suffer harsh punishments—suspensions and arrests—at school.

There is a pipeline from school to jail that we have to turn into a pipeline from school to a promising future. If current trends continue, nearly 70 percent of African American men who drop out of high school will end up in jail. We have to make certain they do not.

REAL REFORM

We must come together with a sense of shared purpose and demand policies to transform this country into a nation that affirms the value of all our people, regardless of race, income, or national origin. We need a criminal justice system that not only protects our people from crime but is also based on justice for all, nondiscriminatory policies, and the understanding that preventing crime is a much worthier approach than punishing for it.

We must reexamine honestly how we police America, and the federal government can play an important role in establishing a model police-training program that reorients the way we do law enforcement. First and foremost, we must develop new rules on the allowable use of force. Police officers need to be trained to de-escalate confrontations and to humanely interact with people, especially people who have mental illnesses. Lethal force should be the last response, not the first.

Every effort should be made to have police forces reflect the diversity of the communities they work in. And that must include in positions of leadership and training departments. We must demand greater civilian oversight of police departments and ongoing and meaningful community engagement.

We must demilitarize our police forces so they don't look and act like invading armies. Police departments must be part of the community they serve and be trusted by the community. Too often, we see local police forces with military-style vehicles and weapons that make them look like occupying armies trying to conquer some faraway country.

We should federally fund and require body cameras for law enforcement officers to make it easier to hold everyone accountable, while also establishing standards to protect the privacy of innocent people.

We must ensure that police departments do not shield bad actors from accountability and that they instead show zero tolerance for abuses of police power. All employees deserve due process protections, but departments must vigorously investigate and, if necessary, prosecute allegations of wrongdoing, especially those involving the use of force. Every death that occurs during an arrest or while someone is in police custody should be investigated by the U.S. Department of Justice.

We must stop cash-starved communities from using their police forces as revenue generators. In many cities, the incentives for policing are upside down. Police departments are bringing in substantial revenue by ticketing poor people for minor offensives and by seizing the personal property of people who are suspected of criminal involvement. When policing becomes a source of revenue, officers are often pressured to meet quotas that can lead to unnecessary or unlawful traffic stops and citations. And civil asset forfeiture laws allow police to take property from people even before they are charged with a crime. Even worse, it is often difficult and expensive for innocent people to get their property back. We must end these abusive practices.

The time is long overdue for us to take marijuana off the federal government's list of outlawed drugs under the Controlled Substances Act. Eight states and the District of Columbia have already legalized the recreational use of marijuana, and the federal government shouldn't stand in the way of states deciding to regulate it the same way that they do alcohol and tobacco. The current federal prohibition means that businesses in states that legalized marijuana often cannot find banks willing to take their money for fear of U.S. prosecution.

We must invest in drug courts and interventions so people end up in treatment rather than prison. We must end mandatory minimum sentencing and give judges the discretion to better tailor sentences to the specific facts

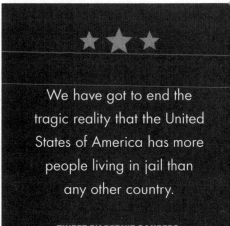

We have got to end the tragic reality that the United States of America has more people living in jail than any other country.

TWEET BY BERNIE SANDERS,
OCTOBER 2, 2015, 11:02 AM

of a given case. The federal system of parole needs to be reinstated because people who are serving long sentences need incentives to make productive choices and earn their way to shorter sentences.

We must make it easier, not harder, for people who have served sentences to be reintegrated into society. They need a path back from prison that will allow them to lead productive lives rather than returning to a life of crime and to jail. People who leave jail need jobs, housing, education, and a real chance to make it in civil society.

Giving former inmates a real chance means "banning the box" to prohibit employers from discriminating against job applicants because of a prior conviction. "The box" is a common element on job applications that people must check if they have a criminal record. Individuals reentering the workforce should be able to compete for work based on their current merits without regard to their past wrongdoings.

And once people get out of jail, their full voting rights should be restored. As many as six million Americans, largely poor and minority, who have served their time in jail were not able to vote in the 2016 election. This has nothing to do with criminal justice. It is a partisan political decision. When people do their time, their rights as citizens in a democratic society should be reinstated.

MOBILIZE ★ ★ ★

Campaign Zero works to end police killings of citizens. Its site, joincampaignzero.org, provides research and reports on police policies around the country, including use of force, body cameras, and broken-windows policing.

The American Civil Liberties Union's Criminal Law Reform Project outlines current justice issues and updates breaking news at aclu.org/issues/criminal-law-reform. As part of its efforts to reform policing and sentencing, the rights group is petitioning the U.S. Justice Department to require police departments to collect and disclose data on police shootings and deaths in custody.

The National Association for the Advancement of Colored People (naacp.org) focuses on disparities in economics, health care, education, voter empowerment, and the criminal justice system while also continuing its role as legal advocate for civil rights issues. Local chapters organize actions and disseminate information.

The Equal Justice Initiative provides legal representation to inmates and help reentering society for former prisoners. Its website, eji.org, aims to educate the public about mass incarceration, excessive punishment, and economic and racial injustice with reports and videos on such topics as children in adult prisons and sentencing reform. It also suggests ways to get involved, including hosting discussions on social justice and urging companies to divest from private prison industries.

LEARN MORE ★ ★ ★

Campaign Zero publishes in-depth reports on many aspects of criminal justice reform on its website, joincampaignzero.org.

Harvard's criminal justice program explores the social context and consequences of incarceration at hks .harvard.edu/programs/criminaljustice/research -publications/incarceration-socialcontext-consequences. In addition to scholarly research, the site provides links to news articles on incarceration, including a separate section on young-adult justice.

The 2015 Aspen Ideas Festival took a deep dive into criminal justice reform with a panel of experts, including a former inmate, and an opening presentation of research by Harvard professor Bruce Western, youtube.com/ watch?v=bZiQtnvAmS8. You can read about Western's work with prisoners here: harvardmagazine.com/2013/03/the-prison-problem.

Pete Brook, a prison photojournalist, recommends twenty-three prison documentaries on his website: prisonphotography.org/2013/11/17/the-20-best-american-prison-documentaries/.

★ EIGHT

IMMIGRATION

REFORM NOW

IT'S BROKEN

Our immigration system is broken. We need comprehensive immigration reform that provides a pathway to citizenship for undocumented immigrants living in the shadows, keeps families together, and promotes civil, human, and labor rights for all.

PATHWAY TO CITIZENSHIP: a system that allows undocumented immigrants who are in good standing to pay a fine, learn English, and go to the back of the line for the opportunity to become citizens

I am proud to be the son of an immigrant. My father came to this country from Poland at the age of seventeen without a nickel in his pocket. Several years ago my brother, Larry, and I visited the tiny town where he was born and raised. While we were there, I was struck by the unbelievable courage of that young man who—with no money, little education, and not one word of English—traveled across the ocean in 1921 in search of a better life.

His story—my story, our story—is the story of America: hardworking people and families coming to the United States to create a brighter future for themselves and their children. It is a story rooted in family and fueled by hope. There is a reason the Statue of Liberty is one of our most iconic images.

Since the nation's founding, untold numbers of people have come to our shores to improve their lives, escape oppression or violence, or flee desperate poverty. More than any other country in the history of the modern world, the United States has been shaped in its identity and character by the process of immigration and the contributions of those immigrants.

Today, there are more than eleven million undocumented immigrants living in the shadows in this country.

More than 85 percent have resided in the United States for at least five years, and many have been here for decades. The vast majority are law-abiding. They have come from many countries, and for many reasons.

Undocumented immigrants are woven into the fabric of our society and our economy. They work in some of the hardest and lowest-paid jobs. Without undocumented workers, it is likely that the agricultural system in the United States would collapse, with rapidly rising food prices and limitations on the varieties of foods we consume. The undocumented are also integral parts of our communities, as they volunteer at local libraries, serve on school PTAs, and coach their kids on baseball and soccer teams.

Today these families are forced to live in fear that their immigration status will be found out. The threat of deportation is never far from their minds.

In Phoenix, Arizona, a group of high school students, some with tears running down their cheeks, recounted how they worry that when they get home from school they might discover their mom or dad was arrested and about to be deported. Never mind that the students were all born here and are American citizens—their parents are not. These kids live every day knowing that their families could be torn apart. No child, no teenager, no adult should have to go through that. Yet today in America, millions do.

A young man serving in the United States military

told me that while he was deployed on active duty, his wife was deported. That is one hell of a way to thank someone willing to die defending his country—our country.

I talked to a twelve-year-old boy born in Arizona who is growing up on this side of the Mexican border after his mother was deported. He told me about being torn between living with his mother in Mexico and staying here in the only country he has ever known.

According to Pew, an estimated eight million unauthorized immigrants work in the United States: 5 percent of the entire labor force. Collectively, they pay an estimated $11.74 billion each year in state and local taxes, according to the Institute on Taxation and Economic Policy. This includes state and local income taxes, property taxes, gas taxes at the pumps, and sales taxes on the goods they buy. Moreover, the institute estimates that they pay an average of 8 percent of their incomes in state and local taxes—which, by the way, is 48 percent more than the 5.4 percent paid by the top 1 percent of taxpayers.

If we achieve comprehensive immigration reform, state and local tax contributions could increase by up to $2.1 billion a year.

About half of undocumented workers also pay federal income taxes, but since their work is often under the table and off the books, they can't collect on their end of the social contract. It is estimated that over the years these undocumented workers have contributed close to $300 billion to the Social Security Trust Funds—for benefits they will not receive.

Meanwhile, undocumented workers are not protected by many of the labor laws and regulations that cover other workers. If undocumented workers experience unsafe working conditions, they often will not speak up for fear of being fired or exposed to the authorities. If they are harassed on the job, they have no recourse. If they are forced to work unreasonably long hours or cheated out of pay, they have nowhere to turn. And for the most part, they can forget about forming a union to press for better conditions.

Now, who do you think really benefits most from illegal immigration? As economics professor Gordon Hanson of the University of California, San Diego, noted, the "benefits go primarily to one group of individuals, and that is employers in industries that hire illegal immigrants intensively: construction, agriculture, hospitality and tourism." The reality is that many businesses,

★ ★ ★

A society which proclaims freedom as its goal, as the United States does, must work unceasingly to end all kinds of discrimination.

TWEET BY BERNIE SANDERS, APRIL 19, 2017, 5:01 PM

large and small, have long used undocumented workers to pad their bottom lines.

Just consider the agricultural workforce. In California alone—where the $47 billion-a-year agricultural sector supplies more than half the produce consumed in the United States—between 40 and 50 percent of the workforce is made up of undocumented workers.

All too often, farmworkers are paid horrendously low wages, exposed to pesticides, and deprived of the most basic decent living conditions. Many of their homes lack clean drinking water. Today's struggle is aimed at providing decent wages and safe working conditions for farmworkers, and demanding that the corporations that own the farms treat their employees with dignity.

In southern Florida, the Coalition of Immokalee Workers has done heroic work standing up for migrant workers who are paid starvation wages for back-breaking work. Most of these farmworkers grow and harvest tomatoes that are bought by fast-food giants and supermarket chains. The working and living conditions in Immokalee at one time were unimaginable. In fact, several labor contractors there had been prosecuted for holding farmworkers against their will. In other words, they were engaged in slavery, chaining workers inside box trucks at night and beating them during the day.

Because of the tremendous grassroots efforts of the coalition, with the support of Oxfam America and dozens of other organizations, working conditions in Immokalee began to improve, and workers received a small wage increase when Burger King, Subway, Taco Bell, Whole Foods, and many others agreed to pay higher prices for the tomatoes. How many more Immokalees are out there? How many thousands of undocumented workers are being ruthlessly exploited every day, with few people knowing about it?

Exploitation of undocumented workers is certainly not limited to the agricultural sector. A 2013 investigation by ProPublica and public radio's *Marketplace* exposed how the Chicago doll manufacturer Ty Inc. used layers of shadowy labor brokers to find low-wage workers, many of them undocumented, for its factories. Since the workers weren't direct employees of the company, Ty had plausible deniability about their immigration status. These workers labored long hours at the minimum wage and then had to pay the brokers out of their own pockets for the privilege of being selected and transported to work. And sometimes they were not paid what they were promised. Of course, they had no legal recourse, no one to complain to. The investigation found similar practices at Fresh Express, Sony, Frito-Lay, and Smirnoff.

Walmart has employed undocumented workers to clean its stores. Tyson Foods has used them to process chickens, amid many violations of laws on workplace conditions and allegations of human smuggling. Many

American families, including at least two nominees for attorney general, have employed undocumented workers to care for their children. Undocumented workers cut lawns, clean hotel rooms, work in oilfields, and staff nursing homes. In my state of Vermont, they work on a growing number of dairy farms. They work on construction crews, and many helped rebuild entire neighborhoods in New Orleans after Katrina.

> Instead of a race to the bottom, we have got to start lifting up living and working standards throughout the country.
>
> **TWEET BY BERNIE SANDERS, MARCH 4, 2017, 12:45 PM**

If we are serious about increasing wages in this country for all workers, immigrant and native-born alike, we must extend labor protections to undocumented workers and stop allowing employers to pay them starvation wages. If we start giving undocumented workers legal protections, we can slow down the "race to the bottom." Wages for the lowest-paid workers in the country will rise, and with legal status, they will be able to join unions and negotiate decent pay and working conditions. A rising tide lifts all boats.

But that would affect big business's bottom line, and therein lies the rub. After all, the political and business establishment in this country is really not all that concerned about immigration's impact on native, low-skill workers—but they are very concerned about profit margins. Let me give you an example.

Over the years, corporate America has successfully pushed for the creation of federal programs that allow employers to bring temporary "guest workers" into the country, supposedly because there is no one here who can do the jobs. Of course, that threshold is very squishy and has been exploited by the business community. When employers report that they need to bring in foreign labor because there is no one in this country able to do their jobs, what is really going on is that there is no one here willing to do the job for the low wages being offered. Too often, guest worker programs are used not to help employers hire labor they can't find locally, but to drive down wages with cheap labor from abroad. Instead of a rising tide lifting all boats, it is a leaky boat sinking slowly to the bottom. But it gets worse.

The Southern Poverty Law Center and the AFL-CIO have documented many cases of employers cheating guest workers out of wages, seizing their passports, forcing them to live in substandard conditions, and even denying them medical treatment for on-the-job injuries. Guest workers will understandably hesitate before complaining because while they are here legally, their temporary visa is tied to a specific company. Their fate is effectively controlled by the employer.

There is a lot of discussion regarding "illegal immigration." There is too little discussion and legislative action regarding how corporate America and the business community exploit and benefit from the labor of undocumented workers.

THE IMPACT OF NAFTA

When we talk about the "flood" of undocumented people who have come into the United States, we must consider the impact of American policy, especially trade policy and the North American Free Trade Agreement. When NAFTA was passed, its proponents said that liberalized trade with Mexico would increase the standard of living in that country, and thus reduce the flow of undocumented immigrants into the United States. In fact, the exact opposite happened.

After NAFTA went into effect in 1994, inexpensive and highly subsidized American corn exports to Mexico increased fivefold, flooding the Mexican market and pushing hundreds of thousands of farmers off their lands. Pork imports into the country rose by twenty-five-fold, eliminating 120,000 Mexican jobs. The number of Mexicans living in extreme poverty surged by more than fourteen million. And the number of Mexicans entering the United States without authorization increased by 185 percent between 1992 and 2011. Free trade didn't stem illegal immigration, it accelerated it.

Proponents of the Central America Free Trade Agreement—which expanded NAFTA to five Central American nations and the Dominican Republic— similarly argued that the 2004 agreement would stem illegal immigration. But prolonged economic instability, some of the worst gang violence in the world, and widespread drug trafficking in Guatemala, El Salvador, and Honduras have sent a surge of undocumented immigrants to the United States since 2014. This includes previously unheard of numbers of mothers with young children, and unaccompanied minors sent by their parents on a perilous trip north in search of safety.

These refugees are fleeing horrific violence in their home countries, and many suffer kidnapping, extortion, human trafficking, and rape as they travel through Mexico. It is deeply distressing to me that so many voices in our country blithely insist that these desperate people, mostly women and young children, should be sent back to the countries they fled. What horrors will they face if they are forced to return?

As a civilized nation, we have a moral obligation to make sure these families and children are humanely cared for while in U.S. custody. But sadly, that is not always the case. The three family detention centers, including the two opened in 2014, are overcrowded and lack proper medical facilities. Detainees are treated like criminals, sometimes being woken up every fifteen minutes at night. There have been documented cases of detainee abuse, including rape. Almost half of all unaccompanied children in custody do not even have a lawyer while in deportation proceedings.

To my mind, the U.S. government should not be in the painful and inhumane business of locking up families who have fled violence. We must put an end to family detention and treat these families with the compassion and dignity they deserve.

We cannot, should not, and will not sweep up eleven million people and throw them out of the country. Tearing apart families and disrupting whole communities is not only inhumane, it isn't close to being feasible. Can you imagine the size and cost of the deportation force that would be needed to track down, arrest, and process eleven million people? Or the number of prison cells needed to temporarily house them? Or the number of planes or buses needed to deport them? Not to mention the incredible economic dislocation such an action would have. Really, the whole idea is beyond absurd.

We need to get serious. We need comprehensive immigration reform.

WHAT IMMIGRATION REFORM MUST INCLUDE

The Congress must do its job and pass what the majority of Americans demand—a comprehensive and humane immigration reform policy. Let me outline what that means to me.

First and foremost, it means creating a path for the eleven million undocumented people in our country to become lawful permanent residents and eventually citizens. It is time to bring these people out of the shadows and give them the full protection of the law. They should be allowed to improve their lives while contributing more fully and fairly to the American economy, including paying their fair share of income, Social Security, and Medicare taxes and then benefiting from these programs at the other end.

The path to citizenship must be fair in terms of not having overly restrictive eligibility dates and application periods. Financial penalties and fees must likewise be fair—they cannot be so onerous as to be an obstacle for attaining legal residency.

Immigration reform must include the DREAM Act: the granting of conditional residency to people who serve in the military or attend college. It's time to tap the potential of all our youth.

Immigration reform must allow individuals to apply for relief, even if convicted of nonviolent offenses. A prior nonviolent conviction shouldn't automatically disqualify someone from legal residency. Done correctly, immigration reform will allow the authorities to appropriately focus on violent offenders, instead of on hardworking people who want to get right with the law.

Immigration reform must eliminate the three-year, ten-year, and permanent "bars." Every year, thousands of people leave the country to "normalize" their immigration status, which, depending on the circumstances, sometimes has to be done from outside the country. However, once outside, they realize that they are barred from reentering for three or ten years, or in some cases permanently, because they were previously here illegally. It makes no sense to bar people—some of whom have been living here for many years—from reentering, only to allow them back in years later. Let's eliminate this catch-22 many people face when legally applying for a green card.

GREEN CARD: an immigrant identity card proving its holder has official permission to reside and work permanently in the United States

Immigration reform means ending arbitrary family deportation sweeps. And it means expanding humanitarian parole for unjustly deported immigrants to hasten the reunification of broken families. The program, administered by the U.S. Citizenship and Immigration Services, allows a noncitizen to enter the country legally for a short time because of family emergency, to reunite parents and children, or to attend civil or criminal court proceedings.

Immigration reform means immediately ending family detention. And it means promoting alternatives to individual detention, which would allow thousands of nonviolent detainees to reunite with their families as they wait for their day in court.

Immigration reform means ending for-profit, privately run immigration detention facilities.

Immigration reform means significantly improving conditions inside public detention facilities, especially for vulnerable populations, including pregnant women, unaccompanied minors, LGBT individuals, and detainees with disabilities.

Immigration reform means making sure all detained immigrants always have access to legal counsel before and during hearings to ensure due process and equal protection. And it means providing adequate funding to eliminate the backlog in immigration courts and restoring judicial discretion to allow immigration judges to consider the unique circumstances of each case.

Immigration reform must focus on cracking down on unscrupulous employers that exploit undocumented workers, rather than on penalizing workers. And it should establish a whistle-blower visa for undocumented workers who report labor violations to protect those who currently don't report infractions for fear of deportation and to hold accountable employers that currently abuse workers with impunity.

Immigration reform must include tough measures to prevent employers from exploiting temporary guest workers. Binding workers to a specific employer or not allowing their family members to work creates a situation rife with abuse and exacerbates an already unequal relationship between the employer and the employee. We can't continue to let this go unchecked.

Immigration reform means making sure our borders are modern and secure, especially in this era when terrorism can come from anywhere. Rather than building walls, we must target construction wisely and invest in high-tech equipment and state-of-the-art cameras. We must avoid the overmilitarization of our border communities and work more closely with local residents and law enforcement.

Immigration reform must create viable and legal channels that match our labor market needs and promote family cohesion. Family-based visas are at the center of a humane immigration system, which recognizes that workers with families nearby are healthier and more productive and that their families, particularly children, benefit immensely as well. Prioritizing the unity of families is a time-tested American value.

In light of a historic refugee crisis, immigration reform means reaffirming our commitment to accepting our fair share of refugees. At a time when millions of people have fled unspeakable violence with nothing but the shirts on their backs, we must do our part to offer safe refuge. And we must make a special effort to enhance protections for survivors of gender-based violence and human trafficking.

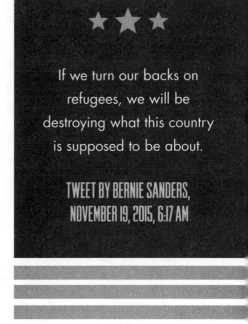

If we turn our backs on refugees, we will be destroying what this country is supposed to be about.

TWEET BY BERNIE SANDERS, NOVEMBER 19, 2015, 6:17 AM

Until we achieve a single-payer health care system, all immigrants—including undocumented workers and their families—should be able to purchase insurance. Aspiring Americans represent a large portion of the remaining uninsured in our country, and allowing them to purchase health insurance with their own money is good for them and will reduce overall health care costs.

And lastly, immigration reform means recognizing that inequality across the world is a major driving force behind migration. The truth is, our free-trade policies are exacerbating inequality by devastating local economies, pushing millions to migrate. We must rewrite our trade policies to end the race to the bottom and instead work to lift the living standards of Americans and people throughout the world.

These are just some of the major aspects of what I think immigration reform means. There are certainly others. But what should never get lost in the wonky details of immigration policy is that we are talking about people. We are talking about families.

With strong moral leadership, I believe we can move our nation toward commonsense, humane, and comprehensive immigration reform. And by doing that, we can reverse the decline of our middle class, better equip the United States to compete in the global economy, and build upon our national tradition of embracing diversity and difference and harnessing them for the common good.

We are a nation of immigrants.
I am the son of an immigrant myself.
Their story, my story, our story is
a story of America:
hard-working families coming to the United States
to create a brighter future for their children.

MOBILIZE ★ ★ ★

The Southern Poverty Law Center advocates for immigrant rights as part of its overall mission to fight hate and bigotry. Its site, splcenter.org/issues/immigrant-justice, includes fact sheets, links to ongoing cases, opportunities to raise money, and stories of legal successes.

The United Farm Workers is the country's largest union for agricultural workers. In addition to representing its members in conflicts with big business, the union supports immigration reform and works to improve farm and food safety. Its site, ufw.org, includes ways to take action, fact sheets on key issues, and the latest news and press releases.

Border Angels (borderangels.org) supports immigrants along the Mexico-California border by maintaining water stations along migrant crossing routes, reaching out to day laborers and informing them of their rights, and providing free or low-cost legal services.

The National Immigration Law Center (nilc.org) defends and advances the rights of low-income immigrants through lawsuits and educates decision makers and the general public about the impact of proposed laws and policy on immigrants.

The National Immigration Forum promotes the value of immigrants and immigration to the nation. Its site, immigrationforum.org, includes an excellent section, found under the "Bibles, Badges, Business" tab, that drills down to state studies of positive immigrant contributions.

The Young Center for Immigrant Children's Rights (theyoungcenter.org) trains volunteers as immigrant-child advocates in Chicago, New York, Houston, and Washington, D.C. The volunteers advocate for the best interests of children who have traveled to this country or have been smuggled into it unaccompanied by a family member.

You can financially support refugees by donating to the International Rescue Committee through the New York Times Neediest Cases Fund, nytneediestcases.com.

LEARN MORE ★ ★ ★

The Pew Research Center's Hispanic Trends site, pewhispanic.org, does an excellent job of distilling issues of U.S. politics and policy. It is a go-to site for a deep dive on many topics.

The Institute on Taxation and Economic Policy ensures

that legislators, media, and advocates know the impact of tax changes on people of different income levels—something that most state governments don't have the capability to provide. There is a wealth of data on its site, itep.org.

You can find TED talks on immigration and the plight of refugees here: ted.com/topics/immigration.

The 2011 documentary *Coyote* chronicles how a group of filmmakers traveled to Mexico to try to cross back into America with a group of illegal immigrants. Not all of them returned.

This (Illegal) American Life (topdocumentaryfilms .com/this-illegal-american-life) presents stark portraits of two immigrants—one a student, one a strawberry picker—describing why they are in the United States and exploring their dreams.

IF THERE WAS EVER A TIME IN
HISTORY FOR A GENERATION
TO BE BOLD AND
TO THINK BIG,
TO STAND UP AND
TO FIGHT BACK,
NOW IS THAT TIME.

—BERNIE SANDERS

WHAT IS "GOVERNMENT," ANYWAY?

The word "government" refers to the way people organize authority to perform essential functions. It usually describes who does what, who has what power, and who is responsible for what. When there is no organized authority, there is no government, and that is called anarchy.

There are many ways to get and hold power. Historically, the strongest have ruled by overpowering everyone else. The ones who claimed to be representatives of deities have ruled by divine right, and the ones who controlled the military have ruled by intimidation.

Today, the Central Intelligence Agency describes thirty-one different forms of government around the globe in its *World Factbook*. Most are variations on these major types:

AUTOCRACY—one person makes all the rules and has absolute power.

COMMUNISM—everyone is considered equal, and private ownership of property or wealth is forbidden. Communism's aim is a classless society.

DEMOCRACY—power is retained by the people, but exercised by representatives to whom the people have delegated authority. In a democracy, the people choose and review their representatives regularly in cyclical elections.

MONARCHY—power is held by a monarch, usually for life and by inherited right, who is either an absolute ruler or a figurehead with limited authority.

OLIGARCHY—decisions are made by a small group of people considered elite based on intelligence, race, or wealth and serve the group's self-interest.

SOCIALISM—a central government controls the production and distribution of goods to establish an equitable distribution of labor and property.

THEOCRACY—a religious figure interprets a supreme being's will and makes laws believed to be approved by that being.

TOTALITARIANISM—the state holds all the power in both political and economic matters and also seeks to control people's attitudes, values, and beliefs.

As a democracy, the United States recognizes powers exercised at the federal, state, and local levels. Some processes are controlled in Washington, D.C., some in state capitals, and others in towns and cities. Religious authority is separate from civil power and is set by church leaders without the interference of government.

The Constitution of the United States and the Bill of Rights seek to balance the power exercised by the federal government with powers exercised by the states and the rights of individuals. In a system of "checks and balances," the executive, legislative, and judicial branches of goverment each use their power to check and balance the actions of the others. The system is designed so that the wishes of the people—the voters—direct the actions of the government.

So, the president can veto a bill that is passed by the House and the Senate. The Senate can reject a president's nominees for Cabinet-level positions, the Supreme Court, and other federal judgeships. The Supreme Court can overturn laws passed by Congress or the states if it determines that those laws contradict the intent of the Constitution.

The Constitution establishes that the federal government declares war, regulates trade both among the states and with foreign countries, prints and controls the distribution of money, maintains and funds the military, establishes postal rates, and determines who can become a citizen. The Constitution also states that Congress can make the laws necessary to carry out these broad powers, thus allowing the federal government to regulate such specific things as the Internet and immigration.

State governments, composed of the same three branches, establish and regulate schools, issue licenses for driving, marriage, fishing, and hunting, regulate trade within state borders, conduct elections, punish crimes, and provide for the public health and safety.

Both the state and federal governments collect taxes, build roads, establish court systems, and charter banks.

County, city, or town governments also collect taxes to maintain police and fire departments, public transportation, parks, and public works such as road upkeep, snow removal, waste collection, and signs.

All in all, the key purpose of the Constitution and Bill of Rights is to ensure that the voice of the individual citizen is both heard and counted through the election process and tripart system of checks and balances. It is up to each of us to decide whether the people who have been elected are hearing our voice. We must insist on transparency in government by holding each and every elected official accountable. When we are disappointed by how they represent us, we must work to replace them.

GLOSSARY OF ECONOMIC TERMS

401(K)—an account in which an employee can save pretax earnings for retirement, often combined with employer contributions; taxes on that money are deferred until the employee makes withdrawals

BAILOUT—a rescue from financial distress with public funds

BIPARTISAN—involving cooperation, compromise, or agreement between two major political parties

BUSINESS MODEL—the plan a company makes to guide its operations that usually defines the target customers, sources of funding, and expected revenue

CAPITAL GAINS—money from selling a property or investment for more than its purchase price

CARRIED-INTEREST LOOPHOLE—an allowance in the tax law that treats the earnings of private fund managers as capital gains rather than regular income, thus reducing their taxes

CENTRAL BANK—a national monetary authority that controls the amount of money in circulation and establishes interest rates for private banks

COLLECTIVE BARGAINING—negotiations between an employer and a labor union about matters such as wages, hours, and working conditions

COLLUSION—a secret agreement or cooperation among parties, usually for an illegal purpose

COST OF LIVING—the price of goods and services that constitute the basic necessities of life, such as food, shelter, health care, education, and transportation

CURRENCY CHEATING—a country artificially devaluing its currency so that its own goods become less expensive and imports become more expensive

DEFINED-BENEFIT PENSION PLAN—a retirement plan in which employee benefits are determined by a set formula and paid entirely by the employer

DEREGULATE—to remove restrictions imposed by a governing body

DERIVATIVE—a contract between two or more parties to make a payment based on the value of some asset or product

DIVIDEND—money from a company's profits that it pays to its shareholders

EFFECTIVE TAX RATE—the average rate at which individual income or corporate profit is taxed

ESTATE TAX—a tax applied to the worth of a person's property and investments after the person's death; it is paid before assets are distributed to heirs

FAMILY LEAVE—job-protected leave given to an employee to bond with a new child, care for an immediate family member with a serious health condition, or recover from his or her own serious health condition

FEDERAL POVERTY LEVEL—the maximum income used to determine who qualifies for food stamps, Medicaid, and other public assistance

FEDERAL RESERVE—the central bank system of the United States set up by Congress to maintain the stability of financial systems, supervise financial institutions, and promote consumer protection and community development

FINANCIAL PRODUCTS—any instrument, such as annuities, stocks, bank accounts, certificates of deposit, bonds, or mutual funds, that helps a person save, invest, or get insurance or a loan

FREE TRADE—unrestricted international exchange of goods without quotas, restrictions, or taxes

GIFT TAX—tax paid by the recipient on any gift above a specified value or amount of money

GLASS-STEAGALL ACT—federal legislation passed in 1933 and repealed in 1999 that prohibited commercial banks, which hold deposits and make loans to consumers, from also being investment banks, which trade in stocks and bonds

GROSS DOMESTIC PRODUCT (GDP)—the combined value of all the goods and services a country produces in a year

HEDGE FUND—an investing group open only to wealthy individuals that uses speculative techniques in hopes of making huge profits and eliminating risk

HOLDINGS—property or assets owned

HOUSING CRISIS—first identified in 2007, the extension of mortgages to high-risk borrowers and a rapid rise in housing prices that led to the financial implosion of 2008, when many borrowers defaulted on their mortgages and real estate values declined

INDUSTRIALIZED WORLD—the collection of countries that have sophisticated working economies and extensive infrastructure

INFRASTRUCTURE—roads, bridges, water systems, wastewater plants, airports, railways, levees, and dams

LOBBY—to try to persuade a person, to try to influence the way the person will vote

MARKET SHARE—the percentage of an entire industry or market that is supplied by a particular company or product

MEGABANKS—the small group of extremely large banks that control almost half of U.S. wealth

MORTGAGE-BACKED SECURITIES—tradeable investments secured (guaranteed) by a cluster of real estate or mortgage loans

OUTSOURCING—a company obtaining goods or services from an outside supplier in another country

PAYDAY LENDER—a business that gives a worker a small loan with expectation of payment from the person's next paycheck and usually charges an exorbinant interest rate

PRIVATE EQUITY FUND—money pooled by a group of wealthy individuals to buy shares of private companies and businesses with the goal of making a profit

PUBLIC ASSISTANCE—government programs, such as Medicaid, food stamps, and subsidized housing, that aid the poor

RATE TAMPERING—illegally manipulating currency rates for profit

RATING—an assessment of a person's or business's financial condition and responsibility

REGULATE—to bring under the control of the law or a particular authority

REGULATORY CLIMATE—how much government regulations enhance or impede earnings growth

RIG—to manipulate or control, usually by deceptive or dishonest means

SERVICE SECTOR—the segment of the economy that doesn't produce goods, but instead provides services that are paid for, such as transportation, health care, entertainment, and recreation

SUBSIDIZE—to give public money to a private business or individual

TAX CODE—federal tax law, also known as the Internal Revenue Code

TAX HAVEN—a country with a stable economy that offers foreign individuals and businesses very low tax rates and shares little information with foreign tax authorities

TRANSPARENT—clear, easily understood, and publicly available business or government practices

UNDERLYING ASSET—the product, stock, or currency on which a derivative's price is based

UNDERWRITE—to act as an insurer and take on risk for loss, damage, or a reduction in value

CREDITS

★ INDEX